Dancing Alone
in Mexico

Dancing Alone in Mexico:

From the Border to Baja and Beyond

RON BUTLER

The University of Arizona Press

Tucson

The University of Arizona Press
© 2000 The Arizona Board of Regents
First Printing

⊛ This book is printed on acid-free, archival-quality paper.
Manufactured in the United States of America
05   04   03   02   01   00   6   5   4   3   2   1

Library of Congress Cataloging-in-Publication Data
Butler, Ron, 1932–
    Dancing alone in Mexico : from the border to Baja and beyond / Ron Butler.
        p. cm.
ISBN 0-8165-2022-4 (alk. paper)
ISBN 0-8165-2023-2 (pbk. : alk. paper)
1. Mexico—Description and travel. 2. Butler, Ron, 1932–   I. Title.
F1216.B87 2000
917.204'836—dc21   99-050478
                            CIP

British Library Cataloguing-in-Publication Data
A catalogue record for this book is available from the British Library.

For Adrian and Alexandra, of course.

I hate a room without an open suitcase . . .
It seems so permanent.

—Zelda Fitzgerald

Contents

Acknowledgments

*P*ortions of the material about Frida Kahlo and Diego Rivera have appeared in *Travel & Leisure, Américas,* and *MD,* all in considerably different form. The section on the Morelia candy market and parts of "The Day of the Dead" were originally published in *Hemispheres,* the magazine of United Airlines. Portions of the Guaymas material are from *Travel & Leisure.* "Agustín Lara" was originally published in *Américas Magazine* (Organization of American States), "The Eyes of the Matador" in *MD,* "The Last American Matador" in *Border Beat,* and "Shopping for Silver" in *Latina.*

I
The Breakup

*W*e were in Acapulco, lounging poolside, when someone with a telephoto lens clicked her picture from the far side of the pool. She pretended not to notice, but I saw her almost indiscernible reaction, that slight involuntary movement, a twitch if you will, when she heard the shutter.

People were always taking her picture. She had worked as a model in New York with considerable success, but hated it. "The meat market," she called it. Everybody was always coming on to her, she once complained—photographers, clients, the ad people. By choice, she hadn't done a professional assignment in nearly two years. You can take the model out of New York, but you can't take away the model's intuitive reaction to the sound of a clicking lens. Nothing, not even the ocean's rhythmic pounding, the warm relentless Acapulco breezes, or the traffic outside along the Costera, could mask the sound of that quick, infinite, and at times unexpected adoration.

Click! Click! Click! Finally she grew tired of the camera's impertinence. She turned away, picked up a magazine, and the sound stopped. "Let's go to the beach now," she said. We always compromised. Beach and pool, pool and beach. I liked the ocean. She preferred the pool. We moved to the beach and stayed for about an hour, going into the water only once. The sea was rough. The red flags were up, flapping furiously in the breeze, and the breaking waves were advancing farther and farther toward that little portion of sand that we had staked off as our own with books, bags, towels, and sandals. Finally, we gathered up our things and went back to the room.

I made an overture. "Not now," she said, "I'm all full of sand." But I persisted. Our prelude to lovemaking was never verbal, but rather silent and simple, a caress, a gesture, a touch, a form of telepathy that was as subtle and unmistakable as the occasional rejection. Despite sand, sweat, and the strong scent of seaweed, she acquiesced. Outside we could hear the sound of the waves as the ocean continued to claim more and more of the receding beach. Fade out to months later—like a sequence in one of those early black and white movies—and our daughter Alexandra was born, in March. A Pisces child, she had the grace and intuitive wisdom of those conceived near the rhythm and sound of the sea.

Adrian was born four years later, on Mother's Day, squawking and squalling right from the start, but he would soon grow into an inquisitive, independent, intelligent child with his mother's blonde hair and good looks. By then, however, the marriage that was destined to last forever fell apart.

There had been good times and, as with any marriage that had once seemed so solid, lots of laughs. Once we went together to the opening of a posh hotel in Cancún, a lavish black-tie affair attended by a score of film stars and Mexican dignitaries. She was wearing an evening gown with a matching gold brocade jacket. Because the evening was sultry, she slipped the jacket casually over her shoulders. Earlier, when she had packed for the flight from New York, she had made sure the jacket wouldn't wrinkle by stuffing several pairs of my jockey shorts into the sleeves. Because she wasn't actually wearing the jacket, she had forgotten to take them out. A string quartet was playing in the lobby, an official welcoming committee was greeting guests, a dozen or so photographers were buzzing around, and of course, that's where it happened.

"Excuse me, sir," said the formally dressed attendant who came hurrying after us, holding a pair of my shorts crumpled discreetly in his hand, "but I believe the lady dropped these."

And there were moments that I may never understand. On a flight to Europe, a woman passenger came over to our seat with one of the current slick fashion magazines in her hand. "Excuse me," she said. "This is you on the cover, isn't it? Would you mind signing it for me?"

Gerta smiled. "I'm sorry. That's not me."

"Are you sure? It certainly looks like you."

"It isn't me," she said again.

When the woman, somewhat dejected and noticeably embarrassed, left, I asked Gerta why she hadn't signed the cover.

She didn't answer, and we continued the rest of the flight virtually in silence.

I worked at several magazines in New York, *Esquire, Penthouse,* ending up at *True, the Man's Magazine,* a misnomer to be sure. While the popular huge-selling publication championed Man and his world of high adventure, hunting, fishing, scaling the great peaks, cars, guns, sports, jail breaks, and spies, its staff was primarily made up of pipe-smoking family men, some of whom could hardly find their way to the office in the morning, much less romp the Serengeti. Because I had worked at *Esquire* (I left when the company went through financial restructuring), I was appointed fashion editor, a stretch to be sure. What did I know about plaid shirts and duck jackets with huge rubber-lined pockets? The fashions found in *Esquire* and *True* didn't hang in the same closet. I also did general editing, as did most of the staff. In addition, with the silly title of "Fun Editor," I was in charge of the monthly joke page.

The editor's office, I suppose in keeping with the magazine's thirst-for-adventure theme, was filled with zebra-skin carpets, rhino-hoof wastepaper baskets, and assorted horns and tusks, as though anticipating a visit from Robert Ruark.

The magazine had a staff softball team for which participation was mandatory. Before a game, the editor changed from his suit to his jeans with all of us standing around in his office. "Macho" was our rallying call.

One day I was called into that African shrine of an office and told that I wasn't doing my share and that I would be put on probation for two months to "shape up or ship out." That night I cleaned off my desk, typed a memo specifying the two weeks vacation time I had coming as advance notice, and quit.

I don't know if my sudden lack of employment had anything to do with the breakup of our marriage, but it certainly didn't help. Going to work in the morning and coming home at night is one thing. Being home all day, trying to set up a workable office, trying to write, and getting paid for it is another. Gerta and I were in one another's space. I could never quite convince her that while I was at the window looking down on the traffic of West 86th Street, I was working, nor could she understand, since I was home anyway, why I couldn't watch the kids. A year went by, and then another, and that's when I learned that she had decided to move to Guadalajara, sans me.

I had come home from a trip to Chicago and found the locks on our apartment door changed, my things moved to the building's basement storage area. Clearly, she was trying to tell me something. I went upstairs and began kicking and banging at the door, determined to knock it down, and then I heard my daughter crying inside, frightened by the noise, so I stopped.

She didn't know how to drive, but after a few lessons, she managed to charm her way through all the necessary tests for an international driver's license. She bought a car with her "modeling money," which she had always kept separate, and informed me that she was going to move to Guadalajara, that she was going to drive there. And with hardly a backward glance, with the bewildered kids in tow, she was off.

I don't know why she decided to move to Guadalajara, except that we had once talked of moving there, as we had talked of moving to other places—Nerja on Spain's Costa del Sol, Paris, Sedona in Arizona, Munich in her native Germany, wherever. Our restlessness may have been the first sign of trouble.

As upset as I was—our separation agreement prohibited her from taking the children out of the country—I had to reluctantly admire her spirit. But that was her way. Our New York apartment was on the upper West Side. Shortly after we were married, she decided that a second doorway from the living room to the kitchen would be more practical. I told her we couldn't make any structural changes because we were renting and didn't own the apartment. I went off to California on a week-long assignment, and when I came back—voilà!—there was a new door to the kitchen. The building's management either never noticed the change or thought it had always been there.

When she left for Mexico, I asked her to call me collect every night along the way so I'd know she and the kids had gotten safely through the day. She called the first night but not again. It took me nearly a week of frantic phone calls to friends in Mexico to track her down. "Why didn't you call?" I asked, relieved at the sound of her voice. "Nothing happened," she said. "There was no reason."

Six months later, I began the first of what would be a long series of trips to Guadalajara—commutes, I used to call them—to see the children. Certain moments stand out vividly in my mind. One was the first time that my taxi pulled up in front of the house in Las Águilas, the Guadalajara community where they lived, and I got out to find my daughter sweeping the walkway with a broom that was far, far too large, as though she were merely playing house. When she saw me, she dropped the broom, not quite sure what to say, or even what to call me. "Mommy, Mommy, look who's here," she called inside. "It's Ron Butler."

Another moment was on my second visit when Adrian greeted me with a plea for candy money. "Un peso, Papá, un peso." The child, who hadn't yet learned to speak when he left New York, now spoke only Spanish. "Un peso, Papá, por favor." I swept him up, a mass of giggles and tousled blonde hair. I dubbed him "The Golden Mariachi" and envisioned him someday with a big sombrero, a tight white suit, and a giant guitar leading a group of musicians through the streets of Guadalajara. " Un peso, Papá, un peso." He cried uncontrollably when it came time for me to leave. Kicking and screaming, he wanted to come with me and had to be restrained. Kicking and screaming inside as well, I desperately wanted to stay.

A father and daughter are bonded from the start. That's just the way it is. Nothing can tear them apart. But a father and son relationship takes nurturing. What kind of a father would I be? I hated sports. The bats, balls, and drums of son-raising were beyond me, I thought. I'd have to take him to ball games, that great clash of steak-fed buffoons. Yet can there be a stronger tie? I look at those pictures on milk cartons or on fliers in the mail of missing children, and so often the missing child and the person he or she was last seen with have the same last name. Kidnapped by Dad?!

We were civil to one another, Gerta and I, polite almost to a fault, but staying with my ex-wife in her house in Guadalajara was uncomfortable for me as well as for her, especially after I realized that Fernando, the shy, amiable, kind of goofy friend who was always hanging around, was far more than a friend. He was living there. At first he conveniently moved out when I arrived on the scene, but later he was just there. The kids could hardly keep us straight, occasionally calling me "Fernando," or him "Daddy," which incensed me.

Finding the arrangement totally intolerable—him in the bedroom and me on the couch —I began to stay at a hotel when I visited Guadalajara or, if school was out, I'd take the kids on trips, so we spent our time together on Mexico's buses and byways.

Alexandra was only ten when we took the train on one such trip from Guadalajara to Nogales, a thousand miles by rail, father and daughter off on a summer adventure. Traveling with a social director of ten who speaks Spanish has its advantages. Within hours, Alexandra knew everyone in our car, who was leaving at what station and when. Thus, as various passengers left the train, we were able to determine where we were. There apparently was no such thing as a printed train schedule.

My daughter's penchant for diplomacy had been evident a few days earlier as well, when I visited her school. Her teacher welcomed "Alexandra's father from the United States" with full vip treatment, which included a rousing rendition of the Mexican Hat Dance performed in the front of the room by my daughter and three chubby classmates. Alexandra did well in school except, according to her report card, for English, taught as a secondary language in Mexico. "You speak English," I said. "How can you have trouble?"

"I don't know, Daddy," she said. "Every time the teacher pronounces a word wrong—she says 'cur*tanes*' instead of 'curtains'—I tell her the right way to say it, and she gets mad."

So much for diplomacy.

The train trip was our first one alone together in Mexico, and in many ways it was the most memorable. I wanted desperately to be an influence in my children's lives, to be with them as they grew up. Under the circumstances, those travel days together were precious.

We had first-class coach seats; the cost for them was minuscule. Our car was air-conditioned and clean. A porter in a starched white jacket and a face from a Diego Rivera painting patrolled it constantly with broom, brush, and mop. He put clean linen slipcovers over the tops of the seats and later, for a few pesos, distributed huge pillows that were as firm and crisp as fresh-baked *bolillos.* The train, filled with a kind of diffuse root-beer–colored light, was scheduled to depart at 8:10 A.M. It left at 8:40. Who cared? Women came aboard to sell cheese and tortillas, and a man came up the aisle with a thermos of steaming sweet black coffee that he served in leaky paper cups. Then, we were on our way.

There were lots of kids on board, and their noise—the whine and buzz of mechanical toys, beeping toy video games, yelps and giggles—was somehow exhilarating; it didn't chafe against my nerves until hours later. Gobs of *cajeta,* a sticky brown candy made from boiled-down sugar and goat's milk, were passed back and forth over the seats.

We were heading north. On the outskirts of the city, we passed abandoned railroad cars on the sidings that had been converted into makeshift homes. The occupants watched us with blank faces as we went by.

In the town of Tequila, our first stop, men came aboard selling bottles and souvenir wooden casks of the town's famous namesake product, primarily produced there in Mexico's dry central region where fields of maguey plants stretched far beyond the horizon.

Continuing north, we streaked through tunnels that plunged the train into darkness and made the kids on board squeal excitedly. We passed fields of corn and cotton soaking in the yellow sunlight, and we passed a coal yard where everyone looked black and a cement factory where everyone looked white.

The train slowed down, stopped, and started again. A cow on

the tracks? *Bandidos?* The train's parlor car had plush red-velvet seats and shiny brass trim. It might have been the very same car that had brought Pancho Villa north to Sonora for the first time, with his band of fighting Indians riding in the cars behind. At one station, a band of mariachis climbed aboard singing "Cuanto calienta el sol" and later passed a giant sombrero for contributions as they moved from car to car. The size of the hat made the day's take seem meager, a mere handful of coins, but the smiling musicians appeared grateful nonetheless. Peddlers cruised the aisles with buckets of ice-cold Carta Blanca beer and steaming green-corn tamales still fresh in their husks.

It was night when we reached Mazatlán. When the train doors opened, humidity and sweet salt-air smells from the sea filled the car with a warm, lingering presence. By this time all signs of formality in the car had dissolved. Blankets, spread out full, hung down from overhead racks to blot out the lights that were never turned off. A row of young, dark-eyed swains gave up their reserved seats to some teen-aged girls who came aboard, then the boys crowded around them in the aisles. Music played on a portable radio.

The trip to Nogales was scheduled to take twenty-five hours. It took thirty, but we were in no hurry. When we finally pulled into the station, Alexandra tarried to say "adios" to some friends she had made. She smiled, waved and, as with all girls of ten, she turned and the trip was all but forgotten.

Another time we went to Cuernavaca. Despite its popularity, the Cuernavaca Racquet Club was nearly deserted when Alexandra, then twelve, and I checked in. A light rain fell, and restless breezes moved down from the wooded slopes, leading her to suggest that perhaps there were ghosts about. Only a few guests were in the large dining room later when we went to dinner. Two bats came swooping in, diving into the flickering candlelight and terrifying everyone. Up to any emergency, she made a sign of the cross with her two forefingers, and somehow, much to everyone's surprise and relief, her sign made the bats go away, swooping out through the same open window from which they had entered. Shortly after, all the lights in Cuernavaca went out, at least all the lights in the Rancho Cortés district, and we ate our fast-cooling meal by the glow of a single candle. Stumbling through the dark, we walked back to our room and made a fire in the fireplace and sat up talking until the lights came on again. We concluded that the bats weren't bats at all, but giant butterflies.

Adrian, not yet six, was too young to go on any kind of extended trips, and I sensed that Gerta was always a little more protective of him as far as I was concerned, as though I might spirit him off across the border and not come back. Once when he and Alexandra were spending a few days at my hotel in Guadalajara, he tripped and fell on his face, causing his nose to bleed profusely. We got some ice cubes from the ice machine, packed them in a towel, and held the pack to the back of his neck until the bleeding stopped. Alexandra, always the surrogate mother, held his hand and wiped the blood away. Adrian seemed more embarrassed than hurt by the incident. Still tiny, he fell down a lot, always trying to reach out it seemed for more than he could handle of life, both of his new surroundings and the emotions that swirled around us all at that time.

I wrote to the children at least once or twice a week. "Why do you write so much?" Gerta once asked me, "They hardly ever read the letters anyway." I wanted to say, "At least they get them. It wouldn't hurt for you to read them aloud." Of course, as always, I suspect I was writing to her as well.

Christmas was always the most difficult time to visit. Once when I was visiting, Gerta wanted a Christmas tree. She had seen some fir trees growing along the center median on the highway into town and suggested I go there after dark and cut one down; she actually went into the garage to look for a saw. I wasn't about to risk a stretch in the Guadalajara prison for the sake of old *tannenbaum*. "No way," I said emphatically. Fortunately, Santa and Christmas trees are no longer strangers to Mexico, and I was able to find a suitable tree at the big produce market. Joy and harmony reigned in the household. Gerta always invited an Indian child or two in to spend the holidays with the family, some who had never encountered indoor plumbing before, much less a lighted Christmas tree.

It instilled in our own children a genuine sense of sharing and offered me a fragile sense of harmony. Like the Indian children, I too would be leaving when the holiday was over.

Once I arrived carrying a small, pink, plastic typewriter, a gift for my daughter. It was unwrapped because I had to take it through Mexican customs, and anything gift-wrapped draws a lot of undue attention. "It's for my daughter," I told the official at the gate. "Para mi niña." He waved me through.

While at the airport in New York earlier in the day, I had run into a fellow writer who had eyed the child's typewriter with far more suspicion. "So that's where all the pearly prose comes from," he had said with a big grin. The typewriter drew similar comments throughout the trip. A flight attendant asked me if the ribbon was pink as well. When I checked into the Camino Real carrying it, the bellmen and front desk attendants said nothing, which maybe was the unkindest comment of all.

But Alexandra loved it, and the next letter I received from her was all pink.

Once, when visiting in early March, I was surprised to find Christmas decorations still up. I asked Alexandra, who must have been all of nine at the time, how long people kept the decorations up. "As long as they enjoy them," she said.

By and large the visits to Guadalajara were pleasant and at times amusing. Because shoes could be repaired so inexpensively in Mexico, I once brought four pairs, all I owned, to be fixed with new heels or soles. When I went to pick them up on a Monday, the day I was leaving, the little shoe shop was closed. It was a holiday of some sort, for the patron saint of soles and heels, I suspect. It was January, and I flew home to New York wearing an overcoat and sandals.

Another time we went to the huge, sprawling produce market outside of town. The big special that day was oranges, a hundred for about the equivalent of a dollar. But they had no bags. We laughed hysterically as we tried to carry them home as best we could, losing most of them along the way.

The big supermarkets in town, with names such as Gigante and

Super-Super, stayed open twenty-four hours a day. To fill the stores during off hours, management often advertised big sales between 2:00 and 4:00 A.M., and more than once we all went down to stand in line with sleepy-eyed Mexican housewives to stock up on specials in sliced ham or cheese. Sometimes we'd trudge home in the dark, munching on hastily made sandwiches.

Through those few early years after our divorce, Gerta and I established a pattern. I was always going to Mexico or through Mexico or returning from Mexico. I crisscrossed the country time and time again, by plane, by bus, by train, by limousine. The limousine wasn't mine, nor, it seemed, was the face I saw suspended outside, reflected in the dark glass of the side-view window. I saw the dry, rolling hills as we sped through the countryside, passing fiestas one moment and funerals the next. Once a group of people was walking along the side of the road, a father carrying on his shoulders the small white coffin of the child he had once carried in his arms.

And I've crossed the country in a red Mustang convertible with the woman who was no longer my wife, her blonde hair tossing wildly in the wind, while I searched for fragments of a life once shared and for an understanding of the bittersweet journey that had brought us there.

Can we ever understand the demons that dance within? Like her photo on the cover of a fashion magazine, perhaps she believed it wasn't her, that we never really happened.

2
Traveling Mexico through Sunlight and Shadow

Nogales

*A*fter our divorce became final—it took several years—New
York lost its appeal, and I moved to Tucson, Arizona, where I
had attended the University of Arizona and had earlier served at
Davis-Monthan Air Force Base. Nogales was only sixty miles south
of Tucson, and I went there often. Crossing the border after the
sun-splashed sixty-mile drive from Tucson still remains both a dis-
appointment and a joy.

All along I-19 from Tucson to Nogales (the only U.S. highway
with mileage signs entirely in kilometers) your senses are assaulted
by vivid scenes and impressions that roll by slowly in the broad Arizona countryside: the Santa Catalina Mountains, San Xavier del
Bac Mission, Amado Greyhound Park, a thirty-foot-high cow skull
(housing a graphic design studio), palo verde trees, and neat rows
of pine trees planted where copper mines once spilled their tailings
onto the dry, brown hills.

The highway winds past historic Tubac, now a thriving art
colony, and Tumacacori Mission. A hilltop sign off to the right
reads, "The Rio Rico Inn for Golf, Tennis, and Horseplay."

Then the border abruptly appears, a newly rebuilt crossing re-
placing the ominous wire fences and the looping McDonald-like
arches that have long marked the international boundary. Several
miles of dark steel fencing extending in both directions have also
been added recently to deter illegal crossings. After so much open-
ness on the drive from Tucson, such stark signs of restriction grate
against my nerves. But suddenly as I approach the border, I can
hear music coming from the other side. Happy music. Music that,

no matter where I have heard it since, has always reminded me of my children.

Most border towns deserve the reputation long associated with "Instant Mexico." Nogales is different. Along with the usual jumble of shops, bars, and cantinas, it has a kind of elegance and a sense of permanence that seems to be missing from Juárez, Tijuana, and other towns that cling to the border.

Higher in altitude than Tucson and located in a wind belt spilling out of the Las Lomas foothills, Nogales is a cool, refreshing, green oasis within a dry desert region long known for cattle, wood, and silver industries. Despite all the urban bustle and confusion of pedestrian and vehicular traffic, roosters can still be heard crowing in the morning.

At one time, long before the *maquiladora* workers came to swell its population by the thousands, Nogales had a small-town, frontier flavor. Refrigeration came late to the local markets, and butchers used to display their meats and chickens out in open-air storefronts where masses of flies swarmed about. Canal Street was the thriving red-light district. Prostitution is still legal in Mexico, but Canal Street is now a respectable residential area, and the numerous bars and cantinas that once lined it have dispersed throughout the city. The red light has dimmed considerably.

Nogales has blossomed in recent years. It has a profusion of good shops and restaurants and a fine old hotel, the Fray Marcos de Niza. The town is a railway and transportation center, and it serves as the major American gateway to Hermosillo—booming since the passage of the North American Free Trade Agreement (NAFTA)—and to the west coast fishing and sea resorts of Kino Bay, Guaymas, and Mazatlán nestled along the Gulf of California.

But more important, the flavor of Mexico has steeped and bubbled here over the years like a rich *sopa de pollo.*

The name Nogales comes from rows of walnut *(nogal)* trees that once grew on either side of the border. Nogales, Sonora, shares the international boundary with Nogales, Arizona; the population on the Mexican side is 250,000, compared with 22,000 on the U.S. side.

The juxtaposition has created good neighbors. Americans cross the border to buy silver, handicrafts, leather goods, and ingredients for tangy margaritas. Rebozo-wrapped Mexican housewives, many married to men who hold permanent jobs on nearby Arizona farms and ranches, cross every few days to shop for groceries and clothes. Theaters on the American side show Cantinflas films; the Mexican movie houses frequently run the latest double feature from Hollywood. Newspapers from both cities cover one another's news events, including daily birth, marriage, and death notices, and it's not uncommon to see fire engines screeching across the border in times of emergencies.

The center of the vast Santa Cruz Valley, once known as "Apacheland," Nogales was founded in 1882 by itinerant merchants. A major trade and transportation hub since the days of the Spanish missionaries, it became a link in 1888 between the New Mexico and Arizona Railroad and Mexico's Sonora Railroad.

Today Nogales is still an important rail center. The Pacific Railroad of Mexico travels the thousand miles between Guadalajara and Nogales in just under twenty-six hours, making it the fastest long-distance train in Mexico. This was the train trip I made with my daughter. I was anxious to show her cowboys and Indians. I also wanted her to see St. Anne's, the small adobe church in Tubac where she was baptized, but she was asleep when the bus passed Tubac.

Good highways make Nogales a major gateway through which huge streams of traffic funnel in and out of Mexico each day. It's this easy accessibility that gives Nogales much of its tourist appeal and has aided its development. This accessibility also makes it a fertile ground for drug trafficking. Anyone crossing the border will find customs and immigration officials zealous in their pursuit of contraband goods and illegal aliens.

Calle Obregón, the main street of Nogales, Sonora, runs north and south through town. At Obregón 1, just to the right of the border crossing, is the Restaurant Elvira, with patio dining and an adjoining nightclub called the Cucaracha. The restaurant is owned and operated by Rubén Munroy, whose brother Hector was once the town's mayor. Rubén, his hair slicked back like a 1930s matinee idol, offers customers an ear-to-ear grin and a free shot of tequila with lunch and dinner orders. A longtime battle with diabetes has resulted in the amputation of one of his legs—at first only a few toes, then his foot, and finally his leg up to his knee. Using a walker, Rubén scoots around the restaurant, treating the amputation as little more than an inconvenience. Longtime regulars tease that he's using the missing extremities in his burritos.

One evening when I came into the restaurant, Rubén was nowhere to be seen. I looked around and then asked his wife Alicia, who was at the cash register, where he was.

"He's gone to the other side," she said.

I was shocked. "I didn't know," I said. "I'm truly sorry."

Realizing from the expression on my face what I was thinking, she nearly broke into giggles. "He's across the border. He went there to buy groceries and supplies."

Feeling foolish, but relieved, I went off to my usual table.

Down the block at Obregón 125 is the ten-story, 100-room, air-conditioned Hotel Fray Marcos de Niza, named after the Franciscan monk who in 1539 was the first white man to enter the Santa Cruz region. He was in search of the legendary Seven Cities of Cíbola. The hotel is the focal point for much of Nogales's social and civic activity, and around it winds a constant flow of street life—peddlers selling everything from "precious" stones to lottery tickets, tourists with cameras and straw hats, young men looking for women, politicians looking for votes.

The town has a number of other hotels (some of dubious reputation). But Nogales is basically a one-day stop for American visitors. Those who do stay overnight generally opt for one of the several good motor hotels on the American side, or they're too much in love with Mexico to care.

Calle Obregón continues in an orderly sprawl of souvenir, craft, and leather goods shops; bars; restaurants; and liquor stores. The leading fashion boutique in Nogales is located here as well. Joffroy's is operated by an old-line family who once sponsored famed Spanish matador Belmonte's tour to Mexico. Parallel streets—Avenida Juárez, Lopez Mateos, and Insurgentes—offer more of the same. But it is the comparative quiet of Calle Elias, a street where fresh white adobe walls melt into the dry brown earth of the hillside, that attracts most Nogales visitors. Here in a huge, hacienda-style building, a former private estate, one can eat at the restaurant La Roca upstairs and shop downstairs at El Changarro, whose showrooms feature Mexican antiques, fabrics, and boutique fashions.

Directly next door are the remains of what was once Nogales's most famous restaurant, La Caverna, which was destroyed by fire in 1963, just after marking its fiftieth anniversary. The restaurant had occupied a large natural cave that once served as a prison. The prison's most famous occupant was the Apache warrior chief, Geronimo.

In the south part of town, out past a cavernous supermarket where everything from home furnishings to fresh shrimp is sold, is the Plaza de Toros. The border bullring season generally runs from April to October, alternating with Mexico's regular December-to-Easter season. For bullfight aficionados, the border performances pale considerably against the major big-city events, but are always spirited nonetheless.

On the road just past the bullring, a small roadside park contains two large sculptures, each about two stories high. One is of the Mexican hero-president Benito Juárez; the other is of St. Michael slaying a dragon. Both are the works of famed Spanish sculptor Alfredo Just and were intended to be placed on opposite hillsides overlooking the town. But the artist died shortly after the works were completed, and no one in Nogales has since figured out how to move them. So they remain, these unlikely companions, a part of rather than apart from the border town they were designed to oversee.

It seems almost right somehow.

I've always liked Nogales, tacky and rundown though it may seem. I guess it's because part of my youth is there. My college friends and I hung out with bullfighters at a time when it was fashionable, dazzled by the sparkle of the "suit of lights," feeling a little like Hemingway, or wanting to be like him. Everything was still ahead of us and, as with the best of friends, our dreams and plans were all shared.

Magdalena de Kino

*L*iving in Tucson gives me easy access not only to Nogales but to other nearby areas in Sonora. About fifty miles south of Nogales on Route 15 is the dusty little town of Magdalena de Kino. Most people who go there are going somewhere else. I was going somewhere else—I was heading for Guaymas—when I decided to stop and visit.

Named after the penitent saint, Magdalena de Kino has a genuine feel of old Mexico—low houses, high sidewalks, storefronts made of adobe brick, streets made of dirt where dogs and chickens have the right of way. I stopped at the O.K. Café for breakfast—strong black coffee, eggs, frijoles, and warm flour tortillas.

If the waitress is busy when you try to get her attention, she'll give you a pert "just-a-minute" sign with her thumb and forefinger, as though measuring the width of a butterfly's wing. But she wasn't busy that day. I was her only customer. Outside, the town hadn't yet awakened. An old Ford pickup truck was driving down the street, scattering chickens and raising a cloud of dust.

Posters and pictures of Luis Donaldo Colosio can still be seen around Magdalena de Kino, some still graced with the faded remnants of paper flowers and white memorial candles. Assassinated in Tijuana after being selected to succeed President Carlos Salinas de Gortari in Mexico's 1994 elections, Colosio was from Magdalena de Kino. (He attended the University of Arizona, giving him a strong local following in Tucson.) After the assassination, a statue of Colosio was erected on the town plaza near the church of Saint Mary Magdalene and not far from the site where, in 1966, archaeologists working with records on crumbling parchment and specialized instruments discovered the grave of Father Eusebio Francisco Kino. Padre Kino was the Jesuit priest who brought Christianity and European farming methods to the Indians of Mexico and the American Southwest, augmenting their crops of beans, squash, and maize with nourishing new grains, fruits, and vegetables. In less than twenty-five years he built two dozen missions between the Gulf of California and the Gila River in Arizona, established nineteen ranches, and made more than fifty major expeditions to gather materials and draft maps for reports to send back to Europe.

Following the discovery, the Mexican government allocated $11 million for the construction of a colonial-style civic plaza around the grave. The excavation, covered by transparent glass panels, lies exposed, exactly as it was found. Near the priest's skeletal remains is a leather-bound Bible. The dome-shaped visiting area is curved in such a way that even a simple whisper is amplified and carried across the plaza. For all its simplicity, for all its bright sunlight, the Kino Shrine has the strength and feel of an ancient holy sanctuary, a place of miracles.

The nineteenth-century church of Saint Mary Magdalene was built to replace the original church constructed on the site by Padre Kino in 1711. A reclining statue of Saint Francis Xavier, Padre Kino's patron saint, can be found inside the church. Saint Xavier was a Jesuit missionary who died in the Orient. His body survived the long voyage home without the slightest sign of decomposition, a factor that contributed to his canonization in 1622. He is always shown in a reclining position to remind worshippers of his incorruptible body.

On October 4, the holy day of Saint Francis Xavier, Magdalena de Kino becomes the scene of great celebration. Thousands of people come from the nearby towns and villages to seek spiritual blessings. Indian dancers, mariachis, parades, food and souvenir stands, balloons, and fireworks are all part of the celebration. (October 4 is actually the feast day of Saint Francis of Assisi, but somehow over the years the days have been switched in Magdalena de Kino. Saint Xavier's feast day is actually December 3.)

Preparations for the event begin weeks in advance, as the excitement and the displays of devotion grow with mounting intensity. Tohono O'odham (formerly known as Papago), Yaqui, and Mayo Indians come with offerings. Many of the pious cross the plaza on their knees. Tourists from across the border arrive with that almost childlike anticipation of tourists everywhere. Children run noisily through the streets.

Magdalena de Kino is otherwise relatively untouched by tourism, and people who live there hope it stays that way. ("I hope the tourists never find us," said one.) The completion of a four-lane divided highway connecting Nogales and Hermosillo, bypassing Magdalena de Kino, now all but guarantees that desired isolation. Nonetheless, Magdalena de Kino's outgoing residents are proud of the Kino Shrine and the famous church on the plaza and are quick to point out directions for visitors.

There isn't much else to see. The Kino Motel is on the south end of town. Phelps Dodge runs a gold mining operation in the hills nearby.

The state of Sonora got its name when the Tohono O'odham Indians who lived there were told by the Spanish missionaries that their river would be renamed in honor of Nuestra Señora de Dolores (Our Lady of Sorrows). The Indians were unable to pronounce "señora." It came out "sonora" instead, and the river and the state were so named. Second only to the state of Chihuahua in size, Sonora has long been renowned for cattle ranching and the production of leather. It also boasts of having produced four presidents—Adolfo de la Huerta, Alvaro Obregón, Plutarco Elias Calles, and Abelardo L. Rodriguez. Their statues line the main street in Hermosillo, the state capital. Had Luis Donaldo Colosio survived to be elected, his statue would have been the fifth.

Before leaving Magdalena de Kino, I visited the church on the plaza and lit a candle, something I hadn't done in years. Later, I visited a saddle shop, a place for men where the smells of leather and polish were strong and the talk was all of cinches and bits and fast horses, and now and then of women, a subject invariably accompanied by shy smiles.

My car stalled as I drove out of town—someone had siphoned the gasoline. A young boy showed up about twenty minutes later carrying a plastic jug filled with gasoline and asked if I might like to buy it. We negotiated a price. I paid him, mussed his mop of shiny black hair, and continued along the highway toward Guaymas.

Guaymas

My beachfront suite was on a crescent of sand in a rocky cove with the plum-colored Bacochibampo Mountains in the background. I like to be close to the sea. I find tremendous peace on or near the water. Oddly, it's the same solace I find in the desert, part of the reason I had decided to move to Tucson. Playwright Eugene O'Neill, professing his love for the sea, once said he thought he might have been more successful as a seagull or a fish. I think I know what he meant.

The terrain around Guaymas is much like that of southern Arizona, only with the ocean drawn in close and warm sea breezes blowing across the desert face. The mountain range's two highest peaks, called Tetas de Cabra (Goat's Teats) are as distinctive to the local landscape as the towers of the World Trade Center are to New York City. Rugged rock formations drop abruptly into the sea or stand isolated in the shallow offshore waters like some great gathering of prehistoric animals. Hills are sparsely dotted with cardón cactus, a larger cousin of the lofty saguaro, and brown pelicans, already a threatened species on the Atlantic coast and in southern California, flap about in reassuring numbers.

Guaymas is known for its fabulous fishing, so on my third day there, though hardly more than a novice, I decided to try my hand. In the early morning, I boarded a large sportfisherman under the command of Captain José Amador. His broad, brown face had seen many days at sea, and he handled himself and his forty-foot craft with such assurance and agility that my beginner's apprehensions quickly vanished. The Spanish, after all, conquered the sea before they conquered Mexico. We spoke enough of one another's language to joke easily back and forth, once our mutual territories on board were established, and the day promised to be pleasant.

As we left the marina, the towering Tetas de Cabra could be seen off to our left. We trolled offshore for nearly two hours and then moved out to deeper waters for bottom fishing. The sun was relentless, but ocean breezes made the air feel almost chilly. The marlin, roosterfish, grouper, sea bass, yellowtail, mackerel, whitefish, snapper, and corbina, for which the Gulf of California is famous, all eluded us, and we finally returned to shore empty-handed. Captain José, somehow feeling that he was to blame, shook his head in monumental disbelief. He asked if I'd be going out again the next day and seemed almost relieved when I told him I'd be leaving Guaymas in a day or so and wanted to explore the town.

Despite rapid development along San Carlos and Bacochibampo Bays, which feature excellent beaches, a country club, several fine resort hotels, and a Club Med, Guaymas (less than 100,000 population) holds stubbornly to its past. But it's also a modern city with a number of high buildings and a heavy concentration of shops, open-air markets, bookstores, pharmacies, and banks.

Two large supermarkets, MZ (Mercado Zaragoza) and MM (Mercado Morales), are almost next door to one another on Serdan, the main street. They're probably the only grocery stores anyplace where air tanks for scuba diving can be found in the canned-goods section. Close by, on Avenida Rodriguez, between 19th and 20th Streets, is the block-long public market, crammed with colorful crafts, pottery, produce, live chickens, and fresh fish.

Because Guaymas has one of the best landlocked harbors on the west coast, it is the hub of the shrimping industry—who hasn't heard of Guaymas shrimp? The sheltered bay, where shrimp boats tie up near the central plaza, is the town's favorite gathering place. Villagers come here on warm summer evenings to stroll along the waterfront or to stop at several small, open-air restaurants: La Copa de Leche, Chichén Itzá, El Pollito, and La Hacienda. Here, too, is the venerable Hotel Rubi, long a favorite of commercial fishermen who don't like to stray too far from their boats.

Not surprisingly, Guaymas excels in good seafood restaurants, and one of the best is El Paradise, just off the main street at Rodriguez and Calle 20. I had seafood soup and a beer with a squirt of lime. Unimposing, like the town itself, the restaurant's pale blue walls are festooned with shells, shark jaws, giant crabs, and mounted sailfish and other marine species. Clean and friendly, El Paradise is filled at lunchtime with local businessmen.

Midway along the highway between Guaymas and Bahía San Carlos, a winding cutoff leads to Miramar Beach, once the region's most fashionable resort area and still a favorite of tradition-bound families from nearby Hermosillo and Ciudad Obregón. Here, the beautiful, old, mission-style hotel Playa de Cortés was built by the Southern Pacific Railroad in 1937, at a time when railroads were promoting resorts to tie in with their expanding passenger service.

Edith Margaret Douglas, wife of Southern Pacific president Walter Douglas, designed the hotel and spared no expense. She bought fine Mexican furnishings and rare antiques. When it opened, the hotel was considered one of the most beautiful on the entire west coast. In the dining room, a parade of white-coated waiters carrying flaming shrimp skewered on swords is still a traditional Saturday-night extravaganza. But sadly, after many owners and numerous refurbishings, the Playa de Cortés shows signs of deterioration and age. For many, the addition of a discotheque was the final blow.

About seven miles north of Bahía San Carlos is Los Algondones beach where the movie *Catch 22* was filmed. The original World War II sets are rather battered now, but the film's aircraft runway is still operational and reportedly is put to frequent use by smugglers.

The original inhabitants of the Guaymas area were Guaimas and Tohono O'odham Indians. The first historic mention of the region was made in 1671 by Jesuit priests. Nine years later, the fathers established San José de Guaymas, one of the many missions founded on their long journey through Sonora and the American Southwest. In 1769, the first Spanish settlers arrived.

In the years that followed, Guaymas was plagued by Indian wars and buccaneer battles. Windjammers plied the south Atlantic and rounded Cape Horn to reach Guaymas with goods from Europe bound for the Southwest. As a port for one of the richest agricultural areas in Mexico, Guaymas became a crossroads of trade. In 1847, during the Mexican-American War, it was attacked by U.S. gunboats and occupied for nearly a year.

During breakfast on the morning I left Guaymas, a photo in the local paper caught my eye. A visiting angler from Denver, Colorado, had landed the season's record sailfish and was shown in the paper standing on the docks beside his impressive trophy. Also in the photo, smiling broadly, was Captain José Amador.

Mazatlán

Mazatlán has something of Rio de Janeiro about it, the essence if not the elegance. The Malecón, a combination seawall, promenade, and highway, rings the city, with a fringe of beach beyond that gently eases into the sea.

Mazatlán could be called "the poor man's Acapulco." It even has cliff divers, only they dive off a large rock. It's not quite the same.

Like Guaymas, Mazatlán's offshore waters rank among the world's best for small game and deep-sea fishing. I stayed at the El Cid Marina—a part of, yet well apart from, the thousand-room El Cid Resort. My pleasant blue and white suite—it was so nautical, I felt I should be wearing bell-bottoms and a striped T-shirt—looked down on the dock where the fishermen unloaded their catch. Here, trophy fish are strung up, weighed, and photographed before they are eventually stuffed in an action pose and hung on a wall somewhere to forever record their struggle.

I like Mazatlán. Its annual carnival celebration, billed by its promoters as the third largest in the world after Rio de Janeiro and New Orleans, draws thousands of visitors. I've attended numerous carnivals, from Munich's spirited Fasching to Carnivale in Haiti.

In comparison, Carnivál in Mazatlán is almost childlike in its exuberance. Its opening night parade is more Rose Bowl than Mardi Gras, with pretty girls and glittering costumes—a sea of fantasy flowing along the seaside boulevard—while offshore, a flotilla of pirate ships, all cannons and fireworks, lights up the nighttime sky.

Without its carnival make-up, Mazatlán's normal complexion is the color of faded paper flowers illuminated with the kind of lighting found in vintage barroom jukeboxes. Even its newer hotels, which seem to be proliferating—Does nothing stay the same?—quickly take on a patina of times gone by. The countless little *tiendas* that line the main thoroughfare are all called "super-markets," no matter how sparse their offerings.

Despite its reputation as a happening, upcoming resort, Mazatlán retains its offbeat, hidden-away flavor. It's a place that Mickey Spillane might use as a background for a Mike Hammer mystery, or that John D. MacDonald might have selected as a Fort Lauderdale alternative for Travis Magee, the "mender of broken birds." The very last writer whose trail I expected to come across here was *The Bridges of Madison County* author Robert James Waller.

A couple of years after the incredible success of *Bridges,* Waller penned a mystery thriller called *Puerto Vallarta Squeeze.* Perhaps he wanted to shake off the earlier work's sticky sentimentality with something a bit more gritty. In *Puerto Vallarta Squeeze,* a down-on-his-luck novelist named Danny Pastor is a chance witness to the assassination of an American naval officer by a hit man. Later, the assassin hires Pastor and his girlfriend Luz (María de la Luz Santos, who has been known to turn an occasional trick) to drive them from Puerto Vallarta to the American border. All have reasons for heading north, and the novel unwinds to a bloody climax that takes place in the town of Copala (called Zapata in the book), located in the hills beyond Mazatlán.

I decided to check it out. Depending on the season and the demand, several buses a day offer sightseeing tours to Copala, picking up tourists at the various Mazatlán hotels and taking them there for lunch and back again.

Some forty minutes east of Mazatlán along the route to Copala on Highway 40 is Concordia, a dusty, 400-year-old village known for its leather, pottery, and handicraft bargains. The state of Sinaloa is one of the poorest in Mexico. There are no soaring statues or monuments to be seen along the way. So the presence of a huge wooden rocking chair in the center of Concordia is a startling reminder to all who visit that furniture-making is the town's main business.

Copala, about a twenty-five-minute drive past Concordia, was founded in 1565 and was briefly known for gold mining. It is a bit more picturesque than Concordia, with its hills and mountains, its lovely sixteenth-century Church of San José, and a square band shell located in the center of town. The streets are cobbled with riverbed stones.

Copala has only one telephone, located in a downtown booth. Anyone who hears the phone ringing is duty-bound to answer it and go off in search of the requested party. Small wonder that cell phones have made such inroads in Mexico, where the national phone company is facetiously known by those who depend on it as "Taco Bell."

I was looking for Daniel Garrison, who owns and operates Daniel's Restaurant in Copala. Attached to the restaurant is a sweep of eleven modest rooms furnished with ceiling fans and wash basins. Robert James Waller, I had learned earlier, had stayed there for a few days while researching *Puerto Vallarta Squeeze*.

Daniel's was closed for renovations, so my fellow tour bus passengers trotted off to the Copala Butter Factory Gourmet Mexican Restaurant for lunch. Meanwhile, I headed down the cobbled main street in search of Daniel Garrison, led by a trio of local youngsters who had volunteered to show me the way. We passed the restaurant, designed somewhat in the shape of a small bullring (it seats 350 and is known for its spectacular banana-coconut cream pie), and continued out back to Garrison's home. Instead of knocking on the door, my little entourage screamed and screeched for "Señor Daniel" to come out.

He appeared, looking not at all surprised that I was there. He offered me a seat on the porch, asked if I'd like a cold drink— "Beer? Coke?"—and sat down across from me. He was in his mid-sixties, and he wore an open-necked sports shirt and flour-sack pants. There was something about his demeanor that reminded me of actor Robert Mitchum. Indeed, they had been friends. Scenes from *The Winds of War,* starring Mitchum, were filmed near Mazatlán. He and Garrison met—certain people seem to have a way of getting together—and eventually became drinking buddies.

I asked Garrison about the author of *Puerto Vallarta Squeeze.*

"Robert James Waller, with a driver/bodyguard, arrived in Copala in a rented Jeep at the height of the July rainy season and stayed five days," he replied. "I charged them $10 a day each for their two rooms—they normally go for $15.

"Tall, thin, silver-gray hair, Waller was pleasant and easygoing. They went from here to Guadalupe. It was raining like hell."

Waller gives thanks in the book's acknowledgment "to Daniel who gave us somewhere to rest in the mountains, in a small village near the Durango road, and told us stories of the Mexican outback. And to the old men of the village I called Zapata here, who lean their chairs against the walls of their village, smoking and resting and talking after a day in the fields."

Before I left—I still wanted to eat lunch—Daniel gave me a copy of the book, which I asked him to inscribe. He couldn't have been happier. Later, when I returned home, I sent the book to the publisher and asked if Waller would sign it as well.

A month or so later, the book came back in the mail. "For Ron," it said, "Go well. Robert James Waller."

Night Ferry to La Paz

A legend dating back to Mexico's Spanish colonial days when the waters off La Paz were rich in oyster beds tells of two divers—one good, the other evil—who were known to bring back the best pearls.

The good diver, so it's said, once went down and brought back the largest and most beautiful pearl ever found. He showed it proudly to the other divers, thanking the saints for his good fortune and pledging the pearl to the Virgin Mother, patron saint of La Paz.

The evil diver, furious, vowed he would pluck an even bigger and more beautiful pearl from the sea and give it to his master, the Devil. He dove into the water from the deck of their boat, but hours passed without his return. Finally, he was thought to have drowned, and the boat left.

But he was seen again days later swimming underwater in search of the big and beautiful pearl. Native fishermen say they still see him on certain days, swimming deep below the surface, his hair and beard long and flowing now, ghostly white.

The old legend came to mind when I took the ferry from Mazatlán to La Paz and watched the ship's bow slice through the warm blue water. Even the pelicans wheeling around the boat seemed to see the ominous dark and light shadows lurking there in the rough wash. Excitedly, they dropped and dove into the water over and over again, as though trying to force it away. I was less interested in visiting La Paz, where I had been a number of times before, than I was in taking the ferry ride to get there.

The 240-mile journey across the Gulf of California from mainland Mazatlán to the ancient port capital of territorial Baja California Sur takes fifteen hours. For many of the locals who make the crossing, it's the trip of a lifetime. La Paz and Mazatlán are perhaps the only two ports of call they'll ever see.

Leaving Mazatlán, the ferry, also named the *La Paz,* sailed directly into the sunset, moving due west along the Tropic of Cancer and leaving behind a backdrop of mahogany-colored mountains whose base was speckled with the blue, pink, and white colors of beachfront hotels. With night settling, the Malecón was as luminous as a string of holiday lights. I wondered how the lights that seemed so dim inside could glow so brightly from outside.

In contrast to Mazatlán, La Paz, with its narrow, tree-lined streets and shaded central plaza, is more reminiscent of central Mexico, despite the sparkling blue gulf that borders it. Its main boulevard winds around the waterfront, wrapping it in a lazy half-yawn. La Paz is Spanish for "peace."

For the moment, my thoughts were not on the city I was going to visit nor on the one I had just left. I was absorbed by the spectacular sunset. The sea welcomed the sun, as day welcomes night, with flaming silhouettes dancing across the rim of the earth.

The *La Paz* ferry is painted pure white, except for a tan smokestack that bellows loudly as the ship passes the islands of Pájaros, Venados, and Chivos, warning small boats to get out of the way and sending flocks of squawking gulls flapping off in all directions.

The 4,300-ton, 340-foot diesel-powered ferry was built in Japan at a cost of $3.5 million and was put into service some twenty years ago. President Díaz Ordaz called it "another special service for the workers and farmers in the area."

Its launching represented the first practical link between the mainland and the Baja California peninsula, a placid enough stretch of water but one that, because of its sheer expanse, seemed to defy all who tried to cross it, including Cortés in 1520. Since the *La Paz,* several other ships have been put into service across the Gulf of California, serving the peninsula from Puerto Vallarta, Topolobampo, and Guaymas.

The bow of the *La Paz* lifts to accommodate 114 automobiles, a procedure that never fails to intrigue the local populace. Captain Serjio Anayo takes immediate exception to anyone referring to his ship as a ferry, however. "It's a *transportado*," he says, his dark eyes flashing his annoyance, "a transport." It has a crew of 105 men and officers and cruises at sixteen knots.

For all his brisk efficiency and crisp white uniform, Captain Anayo doesn't look like a sea captain somehow. A mariachi, maybe, or an artist, a potter, or even a matador.

My air-conditioned cabin was spotless. Orange sunburst-patterned bedspreads covered twin beds. Fresh flowers graced the small writing desk, and on the wall were brooding woodcut prints of villages far from the sea.

Passengers in the first-class cabins had exclusive run of the main deck with its small swimming pool, lounge, movie theater, and large dining salon. After dinner, a group of young musicians with the detached, faraway look typical of shipboard musicians everywhere played in the lounge.

But the place to be on the *La Paz* was not in the first-class lounge but rather down in the economy section, where the smell of boiling coffee was strong, and tequila was poured from clear bottles with a fine, steady hand.

People danced. Stained paper bags hinted of spicy tamales, bulging tacos, and cheese. A mother, no more than a child herself, nursed her baby. These passengers were overwhelmingly Mexican. As the night advanced, many abandoned their reclining chairs and sprawled on the decks to sleep. Others slept hunched up against the bulkheads. The people of Mexico have long known how to make the most of limited space and cramped quarters.

As passengers do on ships, many simply stayed up and prowled about. Young people clustered in groups along the railing, playing their guitars and singing so softly that the sound of the dark water peeling back from the hull could still be heard over the deck and engine noises. An attractive, dark-haired girl with black, almond-shaped eyes smiled shyly as she moved back against the railing into the arms of her companion and noticed me watching.

A slight chill had come into the air, and I suddenly felt unaccountably lonely. Traveling alone in Mexico, or anywhere in the world for that matter, one becomes a voyeur of sorts. I've been content enough in the company of strangers, but not tonight.

Earlier in the evening I had met a young woman in the lounge, but had frightened her off, I think, when I asked her if we had to dress up in order to go into the dining room. In my labored Spanish, it may have come out as "Do we have to wear clothes in the dining room?" Whatever it was I said, she abruptly got up and left.

The movement of a ship on water is supposed to be soothing, but I slept fitfully that night. I kept waking up. When I was finally able to sleep, I dreamed of my dog Elby. Odd, he died a good fifteen years ago, but here he was, alive and well and still chasing bugs in my subconscious.

In the morning everyone was awake with the first light of dawn, if indeed they went to sleep at all. The ship steamed along the Baja coast for several hours before reaching the docking area outside La Paz, at a village called Pichilingue. A giant manta ray, sometimes called a devilfish, broke the surface off to the right of our boat, and now and then a marlin could be seen.

The wind shifted suddenly, and several old men at the railing smiled, nodded, and talked knowingly of "El Coromuel," the name given to the fast-changing gulf winds. The English pirate Cromwell, who plundered Spanish ships off the Pacific coast, was once saved from almost certain capture by just such a wind, and it has borne his name ever since.

When our modern-day Noah's Ark finally docked at Pichilingue, chickens, two goats, a turkey, a sheep, and a chirping canary in a wooden cage along with a huge departing caravan of people and cars rushed off the ship and into the crowds waiting on the dock. There were greetings and embraces enough to welcome the arrival of the mighty *Leonardo* into the teeming harbor of Naples.

As I drove off the ferry, I looked around for the woman from the night before, hoping to explain my remark about the clothes, and perhaps to offer her a ride into town, but I couldn't locate her in the swelling crowd.

The trip seemed incomplete somehow; I was sorry it was over. I imagined that, meanwhile out at sea, deep below the water's surface, a bearded figure with ghostly flowing hair paused briefly and then continued on, content in the knowledge, for the moment at least, that someone, somehow, shared his ceaseless wandering.

Los Cabos

*I*n geological time, the Sea of Cortés, or the Gulf of California as it's officially known, is the youngest of all the seas, created between ten and fifteen million years ago as the result of violent upheavals along the San Andreas Fault. A large portion of the west coast of Mexico wrenched free, forming a new peninsula when the sea rushed in. Now, surrounded on three sides by Mexico and open on the south to the Pacific, its calm surface belies its fish-crowded depths. With its nutrient-rich waters, the Sea of Cortés contains some of the best sport fishing anywhere—tuna, marlin, challenging game fish of all kinds. Add a near-perfect climate and a great expanse of wilderness shoreline, and that's reason enough to put a gleam in the eye of developers and speculators, who view the Sea of Cortés as the future Mediterranean of the Western Hemisphere.

Nowhere is this vision happening with more alarming swiftness than at the base of the Baja California peninsula, where the land and the sky meet in a fusion of stunning beauty. It's called Los Cabos and includes the twin resort towns of San José del Cabo and Cabo San Lucas. Both were established as Spanish colonial missions in the mid-1700s, but by now all devotional remnants appear to have been washed out to sea.

I was aboard the *Sunderland,* a tall ship that offers a nightly sunset cruise out past The Arch and Land's End, fabled landmarks of the Baja peninsula where pirates of old had once ventured. The two-hour cruise was ideal. The drinks were free, or rather they were included in the fee charged upon boarding at the Plaza Las Glorias marina with its fake lighthouse. The crew members were dressed like pirates. The music was fun. Only the captain's commentary over the loudspeaker about the area's buccaneer history broke the mood. Even the seagulls squawked as he went on and on and on about Thomas Cavendish and treasure galleons such as the *Santa Ana*, which sailed these very waters.

By the time the 100-foot sailing ship and the sun had both found their berth for the night, I felt ready to walk the plank. One of the crew members then came around with a "treasure chest" for tips, asking all passengers to contribute. I dug around in my pockets for change. Anything to get off.

Of the two resorts, San José del Cabo is more reserved, more settled. Cabo San Lucas, on the other hand, is one big happy hour, with bars such as Squid Roe and the Giggling Marlin setting the pace. The twenty-mile corridor between the two towns is principally a hotel zone, where building and banging and the carving of new golf courses go on relentlessly.

I stayed at the Twin Dolphins, one of the first hotels built along the corridor. Oil and luggage tycoon David Halliburton founded the fifty-five-room property in 1977. Luggage and hotels, the perfect match. My room was one of those built low along the seaside cliffs. Sit on the balcony and the Sea of Cortés actually splashes up on your toes. I slept with the glass panel doors open at night, sea sounds filling the room.

A couple of days later, I was on a bus heading north for the day to Todos Santos (All Saints), a little over an hour away from Cabo San Lucas. Somewhere along Mexico 19, a sudden squall blew in from the sea with such relentless force that the bus driver squeezed over to the side of the road to wait it out. It's the first time I've seen a bus driver in Mexico look frightened, as huge trucks and speeding cars zipped past us, sending sheets of water high in the air. What with the poor visibility, any one of them could have plowed right into us. Fortunately, the storm ended as suddenly as it had started, and we arrived safely at our destination.

Todos Santos is a mere "toy piece" of a town consisting of 4,000 people, all of whom seem to project an air of intrigue by simply living there. Who would choose to live in this sandy middle of nowhere? Defrocked priests, embezzlers, criminals on the lam, IRS targets, victims of failed marriages? Maybe I should move here, too. The owner of the Café Santa Fé is from Italy. What's he hiding from? There's a budding art colony in town. I'm always a little suspicious of artists who have to go away to paint—except maybe for Gauguin in Tahiti and Van Gogh in Arles. And there's the sixteen-room Hotel California right on the square. Could this be the same Hotel California made famous in song by the Eagles, as the T-shirts, books, records, and souvenirs on sale inside would have us believe? A theme song of sorts for '70s decadence, "Hotel California" was one of the Eagles's biggest hits. I made a note to check. A visit to the library and a few long-distance calls when I got home proved fruitful. "There's a Hotel California in Santa Barbara I know of," said Joe Walsh, who with Don Felder wrote the music. "But the one we were referring to doesn't really exist."

Before leaving the hotel, I bought a T-shirt anyway. Just in case.

Todos Santos was founded by Jesuit missionaries in 1734 and later thrived as a center for growing and processing sugarcane, once supporting five factories. Throughout southern Baja, abandoned mills and soaring smokestacks still haunt the landscape like ruins of some past civilization. The once-booming economy went bust through world competition and the lack of sufficient water necessary to run the mills. Reborn, Todos Santos is now touted as the next Cabo San Lucas, which seems a stretch. Yet twenty years ago, Los Cabos was little more than a dream of what is today.

All the way back on the bus, the song "Hotel California" kept running through my mind. "You can check out any time you like. But you can never leave."

Copper Canyon

I wasn't back in Tucson more than a couple of weeks when I was invited to go on the Sierra Madre Express, a vintage luxury train that leaves from the border town of Nogales and travels through Mexico's fabled Copper Canyon. There had been a last-minute cancellation, and I was invited to go along as a guest of the line.

One of the perks of writing about travel is a flood of such invitations—trips, cruises, hotel openings, and the like, with the understanding, of course, that writer will take pen in hand after returning and write favorably about the experience. Such travel isn't always as rosy as it might seem. You frequently find yourself staying at a hotel that isn't finished, with workers plodding everywhere and wet plaster falling on your bed, or you may find yourself climbing through ruins or across mountain tops, activities far removed from what you're planning to write about.

And you're often locked in with a group of incompatible personalities, traveling for a week or more in a van or small bus. Occasionally, the group will include politicos or even movie stars. The biggest names, more often than not, prove to be the biggest disappointments.

The lure of a free trip and free food can bring out the worst in this type of a group. Apparently travel stimulates the appetite. You should see the way some travel writers eat. "When a writer dies," said Argentine poet Jorge Luis Borges, "he becomes a book." When a travel writer dies, he becomes an empty plate.

I was once on a European trip with a columnist of some repute and his wife. They came to our table one night, sat down, and ordered a bottle of champagne. They drank most of it and then left, leaving me to pay the bill. I was too young and awestruck to complain. When I ran into them again at the end of the trip, they asked if I'd like to share a cab back to the hotel. I agreed. When we reached the hotel—you guessed it—I got the bill again.

Another Broadway columnist asked if I'd take something back to New York for him. "Sure," I said, envisioning the heady experience of dropping off his column at the New York *Post*. But when we got to his room, it wasn't his column he gave me to take back. It was a bag of dirty laundry.

Ah, but then there were women like Amy, our tour leader on a trip through the interior of Mexico. There were moments when the light was right, streaming through the bus window or filtered into a colonial courtyard or shining softly in a darkened hotel hallway, framing her tousled black hair, her long neck and youthful shoulders, her alabaster skin, that under somewhat different circumstances would have made me toss all caution aside, making moves at the risk of likely rejection, and shattering any hint of professional decorum that still might exist after days on a bus. But my mind and my heart were elsewhere at the time.

There were no such temptations on the Copper Canyon excursion, a train trip that showed me a part of Mexico I hadn't seen before—plunging canyons, snow-topped mountains, darkened tunnels, and swirling rivers beneath 400-foot-high trestles. My fellow passengers were mostly senior citizens, by and large a sophisticated, intelligent group with a lively curiosity and an engaging sense of humor. When Martha, a rather tall woman from San José, had to wear a Band-Aid on the bridge of her nose because she kept bumping it on the low door frames and ceiling beams, a number of her friends put Band-Aids on their noses as well, so she wouldn't feel self-conscious.

The terrain when we left Nogales had been familiar enough—dry desert hills, mesquite, and scrub oak, tiny villages built around clay churches with lopsided steeples, cattle and goats grazing in near-barren fields, kids waving as we passed.

But sometime in the middle of the night, it had all changed. We woke up in the morning to find the train going in a different direction—north instead of south, east instead of west. Instead of desert, we saw sweeping views of jagged canyons and swift, chalk-colored rivers. We were in the sierras now, the high country.

Coming from the dining car was the smell of coffee.

There is magic to train travel, a fact that hasn't gone unappreciated by Tucson entrepreneur Peter M. Robbins, who founded the Sierra Madre Express several years ago as an alternative to the Ferrocarril Chihuahua al Pacífico, the Mexican train line regularly serving the Copper Canyon routes. Actually, railroad cars belonging to the Sierra Madre Express are attached to the existing Mexican train and are pulled by the same locomotive. But that's where the similarity ends.

Imagine yourself back in the '30s and '40s, swooshing through the Mexican countryside, and you have some sense of this train. There are compartments and Pullman sleepers, a meticulously refurbished 1946 Northern Pacific lounge and observation car that once plied the rails between Chicago and Seattle, a dining car from the Great Northern Railroad, a crew as polite and attentive as those from days long gone, and a courtesy bar that never closes. Or almost never.

The big-windowed, well-lit lounge car must present a strange picture as, pre-dinner cocktail party in full swing, it whizzes past remote country villages or a peasant trudging home on his donkey.

"Luís, two more margaritas, por favor."

All the food served on board the Sierra Madre Express is from the United States. Each passenger is given a jug of purified water (refilled as needed), and rooms and lavatories have antibacterial soap. ("Make sure you wash your hands," says Perla, the train's Colombian-born tour guide who speaks four languages.) And there's an on-board paramedic, just in case. Our paramedic was a moonlighting Tucson fire chief, traveling with his attractive wife; they had the compartment next to mine.

One of the cars has an open observation platform, a big hit with photographers and those who don't mind the stiff breezes. Passengers on the open deck are warned that they can sometimes get sprayed with waste water from the cars ahead, a hazard inherent with the combination of dump toilets and high-speed trains. The platform car empties almost immediately.

Our first stop on the longest leg of our itinerary would be Creel. From Creel we would retrace our route back, staying overnight at various hotels along the way (only the trip's first and last nights are spent on the train). The leisurely return trip would allow time for peering over the edge of the Copper Canyon, visiting the Tarahumara Indians, shopping, and taking pictures.

Barranca del Cobre, the Copper Canyon, is Mexico's version of the Grand Canyon, only it's four times larger, swathed in dense green foliage, and shrouded most of the time by low-hanging cloud masses that add an eerie, surrealistic note, a hint of *Brigadoon* in the relatively undeveloped state of Chihuahua in northwestern Mexico. Named not for copper mining but for the spectacular copper hues reflected at sunset, the Copper Canyon is one of the world's most extraordinary natural wonders. Miles of deep canyon, untouched in any way by modern encroachment, stretch on seemingly forever from such vantage points as Divisadero, Bufa Canyon, and Areponápuchi. The air is crisp, and the terrain is lush with tropical vegetation.

In Creel, our cars were detached from the main train. We were told to leave our luggage on board and bring only what we'd need for the overnight stay at the Parador de la Montaña, just a few blocks from the main square and the train station. Several passengers commented that the ground was shaking, or so it seemed after experiencing more than twenty-four hours of the train's bumping and swaying.

Creel is a frontier logging and mining town with a few paved streets, but mostly dirt roads, and a population of 5,000, so there isn't much to see or do. Just before dinner, a few local rug and blanket salesmen set up shop in the lobby; the prices were right and business was brisk. Several shops sell Tarahumara crafts, sweet-smelling palm baskets, some crude pottery, dolls, and carvings from soft pine bark.

I bought an Indian bowl in one shop, and while I was browsing in another, the plastic bag it was packed in slipped from my hand. The bowl shattered on the floor. Seeing what had happened, the shop owner insisted that I take another bowl, even though the broken one had obviously been purchased somewhere else. He gave me a new bowl and refused my offer to pay. The gesture reminded me once again why I'm so fond of the Mexican people.

The Tarahumara Indians are better known for their running ability than for their craftsmanship. Foot races that last up to seventy-eight hours are frequently staged. Local ranchers often hire Indian runners to catch stray runaway horses. Tarahumara hunters have been known to chase a deer until it falls from exhaustion. This marathon running ability has been found to be due primarily to a slow heartbeat.

Several years ago, Richard Fisher, a Tucson guide and explorer, brought seven Tarahumara runners to the United States, where they entered a 100-mile marathon in Leadville, Colorado. Running in the tribe's usual footgear, tire-soled sandals, 25-year-old Tarahumara Indian Juan Herrera took first place in a field of 350, finishing the 100-mile run in 17.5 hours and shattering the course record by 25 minutes. The tribe's six other runners all finished within the top eleven.

Apart from being noble runners, the Tarahumara are shy, wear simple clothing—although many of the women retain their colorful dress and headbands—and are among the poorest Indians anywhere. More than 50,000 Tarahumara Indians live in the Copper Canyon section of the Sierra Madre mountains.

Our second stop, late the next day, was the village of Divisadero, only steps from the edge of the cloud-shrouded Copper Canyon. Although a number of adjoining canyons form the Copper Canyon National Park system, the most stunning views can be found here. The Hotel Posada Barrancas, literally on the rim of the canyon, is a bit more rustic than the hotel in Creel. The rooms have wood-burning fireplaces that keep the tile floors warm.

Tarahumara dancers entertained us at a cocktail reception that night, where we sampled margaritas and popcorn.

The Hotel Misión in Cerocahui, where we stayed next, is a colonial, ranch-style hotel where rooms are heated by wood-burning stoves and lighted at night with kerosene lamps. Electricity at the hotel is available only for a few hours each day, from 7:00 to 8:00 in the morning and again in the early evening, which we jokingly named "*la hora del amor.*" As can be seen everywhere in Mexico, someone was always cleaning. The lobby's tile floor was hardly dry before another damp mop was being passed over it. The hotel has its own vineyard and produces a quite palatable white wine under the Misión label.

Next to the hotel is that very mission, San Francisco de Xavier, a historic stone church, with a square-domed steeple and a spartan interior. At the side of the church, a local outfitter offers horses for rent. There are also a school and an orphanage nearby operated by the Sisters of Charity. Included among the students are eighty-seven Tarahumara Indians, who are boarded at the school during the week and return home to their parents on weekends.

The Mother Superior, with her no-nonsense smile and voice that was soft and commanding at the same time, took some of us on a tour of the school, through the dining room where the tables were set for lunch and the dormitory where the beds were made with crisp uniformity. Classes were in session, and we could hear students rhythmically repeating lessons.

"Is there anything the school needs?" someone asked. "Anything we could send you?"

"Crayons," said the Mother Superior. "Crayons and marker pens."

The rail line through the Copper Canyon began as the dream of a young American engineer, Albert Owen, who in 1872 envisioned a railway shortcut from Kansas to Topolobampo on the Pacific coast of Mexico. Compared with the traditional "Gateway to the Orient" route via San Francisco, the new route would save more than 400 miles of land travel. But the dream dissolved when financing couldn't be arranged. Arthur Edward Stilwell, a noted railroad builder, picked up on the idea in 1900, raised the capital, and began the vast undertaking. But the Mexican Revolution ended that chapter.

By 1930 only the rail line to Creel had been completed. A decade later, the Mexican government bought the railroad and began building the grades, tunnels, and bridges that exist today. Completed in 1961 at a cost of more than $90 million, the route crosses thirty-nine bridges and plunges through eighty-six tunnels.

Filet mignon steaks were served on our final night on the train, as we headed back to Nogales. There, a bus would meet the train for the ride across the border and back to Tucson, where the tour group would disperse to hotel stay-overs, airport departures, or whatever other plans had been made for the termination of our railroad odyssey.

My kids were on my mind during the entire trip, more so even as I crossed the border, returned to Tucson, and faced my empty house there.

Monterrey

My reason for going to Monterrey was mainly to track down artist Julio Galán, considered the newest rage in Mexican art. I also wanted to visit this boom city set against the broad Sierra Madre mountains in northern Mexico. Julio Galán's large, monumental canvases are likened by critics to those of Frida Kahlo and Salvador Dalí. An exhibit of his work was being shown at Monterrey's spectacular new Museum of Contemporary Art, MARCO. I hoped to interview Galán, or at least to meet him and learn enough about him to set the groundwork for a later interview. That was easier said than done.

Galán was having "family problems" and was unavailable, said MARCO's public relations director. She promised she would keep trying to reach him. I wandered through the exhibit of his paintings, a ten-year retrospective, the largest collection of his work ever mounted. They were overwhelming. Most were self-portraits that included personal possessions or other items attached directly to the canvas—long-stemmed roses, photos, mirrors, strips of wallpaper, newspaper clippings, paper-doll cut-outs, bits of statuary. The artist uses this collage of items to snare the viewer into becoming a participant in the creative process. Like Frida Kahlo's art, Galán's work is influenced by Mexican folk art, *retablos,* and votive paintings—flat executions done in bright, vibrant colors. To narrate the agony of self-discovery, he uses figures of himself, often dressed as women such as Nefertiti or some Oriental priestess, or faceless wooden carnival cut-outs. The figures are frequently suspended, floating in space, defying all forces of gravity and reality. "I'm addicted to myself," reads the inscription on one of his paintings. The viewer comes away from a Galán exhibit both exhilarated and exhausted.

Galán, born in Múzquiz, Coahuila, has lived in Monterrey since the age of ten, except for six years (1984–1990) in New York City. He tends to distance himself from other Mexican painters and, indeed, from the public itself. For the opening of the MARCO exhibit, he arrived dressed as Abraham Lincoln, complete with a stovepipe hat. Months later, when the show was moved to the Museum of Modern Art in Mexico City and his appearance at the opening-night reception was ballyhooed with much advance publicity, he failed to show up at all.

As home to Mexico's most internationally recognized young painter and with the opening of MARCO in 1991, Monterrey is rapidly eclipsing Mexico City as Mexico's leading art center. More than half the art sold in Mexico today is sold in Monterrey.

Perhaps the main reason art lovers are attracted here is MARCO, Monterrey's spectacular Museum of Modern Art. Five years in the building, MARCO is a creation of revolutionary architect Ricardo Legorreta. He is a disciple of the late Luis Barrigan, whose designs involved spacious rooms, natural light, plenty of open space, and expanses of brilliant color. "The sky is the true facade of a house," said Barrigan, who even after his death seems to be calling the shots for the look and design of architecture in modern Mexico. Legorreta also designed the celebrated Camino Real Hotel in Mexico City.

The $11 million MARCO has two floors, each with eleven huge, well-lighted exhibit rooms drawing viewers along from one to the next. In the lobby, cascading water fills a sunken patio every fifteen minutes (properly refrigerated, it could probably become northern Mexico's first indoor ice-skating rink). MARCO is located in the heart of the city, near the Cathedral.

Monterrey's other major art museum, the Museo de Monterrey, opened in 1977. It's housed in a former brewery. Passing through an ivy-covered facade, visitors enter a grand lobby that leads to ten exhibit halls where classic works by Rivera, Orozco, Siqueiros, Tamayo, and Dr. Alt are on permanent display. Huge barrels that once held beer during the fermenting period frame the doorway to the cafeteria, where several great beer vats, all polished and gleaming, still stand. For the Museo de Monterrey, Julio Galán created his personal interpretation of Mexico's sacred Altar of Dolores.

Monterrey, the capital of Nuevo León in the northeast corner of Mexico, is the nation's third largest city. It's a prosperous industrial center (steel, glass) with lots of good shops, shopping malls, fine restaurants, museums, and stylish modern architecture. The fact that it's so easy to get to, only an hour's flight from Houston or a three-hour drive from the border at Nuevo Laredo, adds to its appeal.

One of the many mountains surrounding Monterrey, Cerro de la Silla (Saddle Mountain), serves as its unofficial symbol and major landmark. According to legend, its double peaks were formed by Hurikan, the god of winds, who transformed his horse into a mountain to forever guard his favorite valley.

Beer, meat, and bullfighting characterize the city as much as its industrial prowess and showy architecture—at night a powerful green laser flicks across the sky from atop a soaring, red, 250-foot-high concrete tower at the city's center like some futile call to Batman. Monterrey is home to one of the oldest and largest beer companies in Mexico, the Cuauhtémoc Brewery, producer of Carta Blanca, Superior, Dos Equis, and other popular brands. Free tours of the brewery are offered. On the premises are the Mexican Baseball Hall of Fame (featuring Fernando Valenzuela, among others), a sports museum, an art gallery, and a beer garden where sudsy samples are dispensed.

When the brewery was founded in 1894, Monterrey had only 100 blocks of narrow streets with a few shops selling hats, clothes, boots, and hardware; a meat market; and some grocery stores. The brewery's rapid growth mirrors that of the city, which today has a population of 3.5 million.

The manufacture of glass for beer bottles gave birth to the city's thriving glass industry, which now produces some of the finest crystal in North and Central America.

Highlighting Monterrey's position as Mexico's industrial capital is Cintermex, the city's international trade center. It opened in 1991 as the cornerstone of a massive commercial and recreational complex called Fundicora Park. The $30 million center, its soaring interior vaguely reminiscent of the Pompidou Art Center in Paris, hosts trade shows and conventions from all over the world. Its directors were literally dancing in the aisles with the recent passage of NAFTA. Monterrey's proximity to the United States makes it a key benefactor of the new trade agreement. While touring the center, I visited a food and supermarket exposition, a shopper's fantasy come true. Hundreds of dealers and manufacturers were handing out free samples—bags of tortilla flour, packets of instant hot chocolate mix, salsa, spices, cookies, cans of pudding, and new flavors of ice cream. There were shrimp dips and jalapeño peppers, and pretty girls wearing silk sashes proclaiming the wonders of coffee El Marino.

In the middle of it all, a beer company had set up a gigantic gyroscope-like contraption. One after another, volunteers were strapped in and spun around in about five different directions at once, hair standing on end and money flying out of their pockets. I was invited to give it a try, but settled for a cocktail sausage instead.

The next day I visited Cola de Caballo (Horsetail Falls) for a picnic with some friends—chicken, huge *bolillos* (rolls) stuffed with ham and cheese, fruit, chips, and cakes. Twenty miles south of the city, off Highway 15, Horsetail Falls is a graceful, woodsy area with picnic tables, fireplaces, and a constant tableau of families enjoying themselves as diffuse light from the afternoon sun shimmers through the leaves.

About a mile from the picnic site, the spectacular triple-tiered falls cascade eighty feet down over the rocks, creating misty silver highlights. Visitors can walk to the falls or rent horses for the short ride there and back. The riding trail has been thoughtfully located on one side of the stream while the foot trail is on the other, so pedestrians won't encounter any horse droppings.

Monterrey has two bullrings, the Plaza Monumental in town and the Plaza Cadereyta on the outskirts, and they're always full. Elroy Cavazos, Mexico's reigning matador, is a native son. Accompanied by his wife and children and a crowd of fans, he was on his way to church one Sunday, when the fellow I was with, who knew him and knew of my interest in bullfighting, stopped and introduced us. Cavazos, who draws sellout crowds at the Plaza Monumental as well as in Mexico City, appeared to be about five foot one, but filled with all that matador bravado and swagger, he seemed larger than life. I had seen him fight several times and liked the way he handled his banderillas—one in each hand, his arms outstretched, he would make small circles in the sand, like a child imitating an airplane.

Bullfighting is the theme of one of Monterrey's landmark restaurants, El Tio (Uncle), which has vintage photos and posters everywhere. Its specialty is *cabrito* (roast kid). A local bullfighting aficionado, Rodrico Velarde opened the restaurant in 1931. It's now run by his sons.

Another reflection of Monterrey's meaty diet is the Wall Street steakhouse, located in the new five-star hotel, Fiesta Americana. I found myself having dinner there on my final night in Monterrey with a group of big-shots from the local tourist industry. The waiter wheeled a tray of meat selections to our table, and one by one he picked up a sixteen-ounce sirloin, a two-pound porterhouse, a rib-eye, a New York cut, a filet mignon (for two), a rib roast, and slabs of roast beef, explaining the appeal and texture of each, much the way dessert-cart waiters introduce their selections of chocolate cakes and tarts. On the walls were mural-sized paintings of the Brooklyn Bridge and New York's financial district. The evening promised to be steeped in statistics and business chatter. But this was Mexico. By the end of the meal, the restaurant's featured guitar player was at the table, and Jesús Franco, director general of Cintermex, the city's huge new convention center, was singing a duet—and not at all badly—with pretty, dark-eyed Alicia Teissier, a municipal events coordinator.

I was leaving in the morning, so when I got back to my hotel after dinner, I checked to see if Julio Galán had called, as I was told he might. He hadn't. Our meeting, the interview with Abraham Lincoln himself, would have to wait until another time.

Zacatecas

Mexico's showy beaches never lost their appeal, but somewhere in my travels across the country, I had begun to appreciate the interior cities more, especially the colonial towns where narrow walkways and shaded plazas are reminiscent of days gone by. They offer great peace. Zacatecas is one such town.

A pink dust blows down from the twin mountain ranges that shelter the ancient mining town, followed by a sudden shower, raindrops hitting the earth like little puffs of gunfire.

The pink dust comes from the rose-colored stone quarried nearby and used over the centuries to build the baroque churches and colonial buildings that give this city of 110,000, some 200 miles northwest of Guadalajara, its ancient, treasured look. At an altitude of 8,000 feet, with the mountains rising even higher, the setting couldn't be more spectacular.

From my room at the hotel Quinta Real, I looked down on the empty Plaza de Toros de San Pedro, built in 1866 and believed to be the oldest permanent bullring in the New World. No longer in use, it's incorporated into the design of the hotel, with the open bullring forming the Quinta Real's central courtyard.

Part of the bullring's coliseum-like seating area contains the hotel restaurant's outdoor tables, set into double tiers. Large planters with geraniums have been decoratively placed along the step-like rows of seats so that hotel guests, awed by the novelty of it all, don't go tumbling off into oblivion.

Floodlights bathe the arena at night with soft puddles of illumination. Jewelry, art, and upscale souvenir shops surround the ring at ground level, utilizing what used to be the bullring's private boxes, while the grotto-like bull pens are now a bar and lounge area that doubles as a wedding chapel.

The lobby and upper rooms ring the periphery of the arena. The bullring is built at the bottom of a hill and the hotel is built into the hill's slope, creating a uniquely harmonious design. The city's ancient aqueduct, rising above the bullring and seeming almost a part of it, adds yet another dimension. With a five-star rating and a proud listing in *Ripley's Believe It or Not,* the Quinta Real is easily one of the most unique and one of the finest hotels in Mexico.

From the shelter of my room, I watched the large rain pellets explode on the floor of the bullring, tiled over in a rosette pattern when the hotel was built in 1990. Where Ponciano Díaz, Lino Zamora, Epifanio del Rio, and other great bullfighters of the past century once performed, the likes of Plácido Domingo now take center stage for charity concerts.

It had been a busy day. I turned down an invitation to ride the funicular from the top of La Bufa—the city's landmark mountain, so-named because its shape resembles a Spanish wineskin, or *bufa*— out across the top of the city. I don't like heights.

Then, foolishly, I accompanied a couple of photographer friends who thought it would be a great idea to take pictures from the top of the bell tower of the Santo Domingo church. The church was completed in 1750, and I'm sure we were among the first to venture to its summit for less than spiritual purposes.

We got permission to enter the bell tower from the caretaker, who opened the door to a stairway that led up past the choir loft and followed a winding stairwell whose steps got smaller and smaller as we ascended.

I was carrying a tripod and one of the camera bags. The final step-off was scarcely larger than the size of a normal foot. From there we hopped over onto the roof, from which cherubs and gargoyles looked out over the city's rooftops and satellite dishes, clotheslines and street traffic.

The rope attached to the huge church bell, after maybe a million or more calls to worship, was frayed and weathered. The photographers decided that the noonday light was too flat and hazy for worthwhile photographs, so like mountain goats, they went back down the bell tower steps.

But I froze. The top step seemed even smaller now, and there was nothing to hold on to for balance. I started to step off, but pulled back. I tried again. Then I turned around and attempted to step off backwards. Daunted again. I had visions of being evacuated by helicopter from the top of the roof. I wondered it they took American Express.

Sensing I was in trouble, one of the photographers called up to me, "Don't drop the cameras."

I put my hand against the interior wall of the bell tower for support, and bits of plaster fell down into the winding stairwell. Finally, I held my breath and just did it.

"What took you so long?" my friends asked, back in the church vestibule. "If we don't hurry, we're going to miss lunch."

The major church in Zacatecas—and I didn't climb this one—is the 240-year-old Zacatecas Cathedral. It's considered one of the most beautiful in Mexico with its rose-hued facade intricately carved into curlicues and saints. Cathedrals traditionally face a plaza, but this one is right off a downtown street, where visitors can step easily from the city's cosmopolitan bustle into its darkened sanctuary. The cathedral's interior is surprisingly sparse. Its gold and silver treasures were plundered over the years by marauders. Even in pre-Hispanic times, Zacatecas was a stopover along a path through the mountains used by bands of warriors or traders heading north or south. It remained a strategic location throughout much of Mexico's tumultuous history. In 1914, during the Mexican Revolution, Pancho Villa captured the city, defeating a stronghold of 12,000 *federales*.

The movie, *The Last Gringo,* filmed in and around Zacatecas, captures much of the flavor of that period. The film's stars, Gregory Peck, Jane Fonda, and Jimmy Smits, stayed at the Quinta Real, where the Presidential Suite overlooking the bullring rents for $600 a day.

After lunch, I explored some of the city's many art museums.

For anyone who enjoys Mexican art, Zacatecas offers a royal smörgasbord of treasures. Ten minutes from downtown, the partially restored sixteenth-century temple of San Francisco houses the Rafael Coronel Museum, with its spectacular collection of ceremonial masks. Some 3,000 masks made of carved wooden, polychrome, and papier-mâché are displayed in room after room. The masks are grouped by style and origin—bearded conquistador masks, black masks from Oaxaca, devil masks, animal masks. Some have human hair and teeth, others have horns and horsetail beards. All stare back at the starer. An additional 3,000 masks are in storage. Also on display is a collection of puppets from the Rosete Aranda company, the delight of Mexican children since the mid-nineteenth century. The puppets form picturesque scenes of everyday life from various periods in history.

Rafael Coronel and his brother Pedro, who also has a museum in Zacatecas, were both accomplished artists born into a family of great wealth. The Pedro Coronel Museum, next to the Santo Domingo Church, features the artist's paintings and sculptures as well as the works of Picasso, Dalí, Braque, Chagall, and others. The museum also houses an outstanding collection of African art and artifacts. Pedro is married to Diego Rivera's daughter Ruth and has a home in San Miguel de Allende.

In the 1940s, Zacatecas was the second largest city in New Spain, with more than fifty silver mines in operation. When not enough Indians could be forcibly recruited to work the mines, African slaves were imported.

Today, cultural remnants of the past—Indian, African, Spanish, and French—are fused to give this city an old-world charm. Touring the city, one quickly gets the sense that one has stumbled into the high-rent district, so to speak, and it's not surprising. Zacatecas, capital of the state of Zacatecas, has a look of prosperity with its clean flagstone streets, well-dressed people, new cars, aristocratic homes with forged balconies and window grills, and Spanish colonial buildings preserved and cared for like treasured family keepsakes.

A former governor's residence, located just up the hill from the

Quinta Real, houses the Goitia Museum, yet another museum celebrating the works of yet another renowned local artist, Francisco Goitia. A superb draftsman, Goitia (1882–1960) studied in Europe but returned to Mexico to fight alongside Pancho Villa. He appeared to be a formidable foe, with wildly flowing hair and beard (according to the self-portrait on display). Works by other regional artists are also displayed here.

The gardens, fountains, and grounds surrounding the museum are impressive, too. I was fascinated with the way the Mexican gardener watered the lawn—just sort of leaning back, blending in, so that even an act as simple as watering the plants became part of a larger landscape. That's how I water my lawn now. People slow their cars when driving by to watch me.

From the Goitia Museum I walked to El Mercado for a *café con leche.* A complex of stylish shops, boutiques, and restaurants built over an existing daily marketplace, the Gonzales Ortega Market has dramatic French-style wrought-iron columns forming its upper-level streetside facade. It and the ornate Calderón Theater, opposite, built during the lengthy reign of President Porfirio Díaz, form the center of the city's social and cultural tradition.

Despite the elegance of Zacatecas, mining shapes the character of the city. Mining car tours deep into the El Edén Mine, once one of the richest in Mexico, are popular, as is El Malacate, a discotheque located 700 feet underground, still noisy nonetheless.

The mine workers inspired the city's famous *callejoneadas,* or street bands, who lead revelers through the narrow, twisting alleys and byways of the city, playing up a storm. The steady beat of the bass drum recalls the rhythmic clang of the miner's hammer.

Anyone can hire a band from the dozens available, but it's usually the city fathers honoring visiting dignitaries or special tour groups who pick up the $100-an-hour tab to hire popular street bands such as Banda Macho or U-15. To ensure that everyone has a good time, ample supplies of tequila or mescal are available. If the group of marchers is large enough, there'll be a burro carrying a keg of Tequila Sauza or José Cuervo on its back.

The group I joined up with on my final night in Zacatecas met in Alameda Park in front of the statue of Governor Francisco Garcia (during whose term the park was commissioned). Our band was composed of four trumpets, three trombones, a snare drum, and a bass drum, and to the spirited beat of the "March of Zacatecas," we took off promptly at 8:00 P.M.

We went up flights of stone steps, down hilly alleyways, across wide plazas, and through the busy downtown area, attracting huge crowds of people and bringing traffic to a standstill. We made stops at Plaza Goitia, the Gonzalez Ortega Market, and the Saint Augustine Church for libations. But as the band continued to play, off we'd go again. Because of the city's 8,000-foot altitude and with all those hills and stairways to climb, I was doing more huffing and puffing than the trombone player.

The bass drum player, who wore thick glasses to begin with, couldn't see the ground past his huge drum. Though he never totally lost his footing, he tripped and stumbled several times, sending everyone into hysterical giggles. The lead trombone player, poking his trombone into an open ground-floor bedroom window, blasted its occupant clear out of dreamland.

Finally we ended up at a small plaza on the far side of town, where a picnic-style buffet dinner was served in the moonlight.

At the airport the next morning, I was already making plans to come back. I watched a girl lace her fingers behind her head as if to cradle it, then finger her short black hair in a way that suggested it might recently have been cut. Nearby was a man not much older than I who was trying to read the morning paper, but his two small children, a boy and a girl, were crawling all over him. He was almost oblivious to them, except that while one hand held the paper, the other was positioned so that neither child would fall to the floor. He turned the page and continued reading until our flight was called.

Mummies of Guanajuato

Guanajuato is a marvelous old Spanish colonial city in the heart of central Mexico—marvelous in its sense of history, its brooding Moorish architecture, its precarious grace. It hangs on the slopes of a deep rugged canyon, as if ready to tumble at any moment into a pile of timeless rubble.

Gone in such an unfortunate event would be the University of Guanajuato, one of Mexico's finest schools of theater and music. Gone would be the glittering, ornate Teatro Juárez with its stately columns and rococo interior, upon whose stage have appeared Leonard Bernstein, the Bolshoi Ballet, and Enrico Caruso. Gone would be the Don Quixote Museum and the handsome two-story home on Calle Positos where artist Diego Rivera was born on December 8, 1886.

Gone, too, would be the Museo de las Momias, the Mummy Museum. For many, and surely for the 124 shriveled, grotesque individuals on display inside, Guanajuato and the Mummy Museum are synonymous. During special holiday weekends, as many as 4,000 of the living come to visit the dead. Only the National Museum of Anthropology in Mexico City draws more visitors.

Waiting in line in the Disney World–style grid of metal railings used to control the crowd, I was impressed, as I had been on an earlier visit, with the festive attitude of the crowd waiting to get in. People were smiling, joking, and taking one another's photographs, while peddlers hawked candy skulls and *calaveras,* papier-mâché skeletons, much the way programs and souvenir pennants are sold at baseball games at Yankee Stadium. During the harvest season, juicy fresh strawberries are sold here as well.

I had seen the mummies before, but I had heard that the exhibit had been spruced up recently in response to a persistent flood of complaints from tourists. People (Americans in particular) had registered their displeasure all the way to the president of Mexico and the Pope in Rome, expressing shock at such flagrant disrespect of the dead. The human bodies had been on display like eerie sideshow mannequins. I wanted to see the "improvements" for myself.

The exhibition of mummified remains in Guanajuato dates back to 1865, when the first bodies were exhumed from the crowded municipal cemetery to make room for newcomers. At the time, it was common practice to remove a body from a grave after five years if by then the gravesite hadn't been paid for in full. (The law was amended in 1958, prohibiting the removal of interred bodies, space paid for or not.)

As it turned out, the exhumed bodies were discovered to be almost perfectly preserved due to chemical properties of the local earth and to the dryness of the area. Many of the corpses still bore the shocked expressions and tortured gestures registered at the moment of death.

Learning of the phenomenon, crowds of the curious began turning up at the cemetery. It didn't take local entrepreneurs long to realize that they had something special on their hands. The mummies were put on display in the catacombs beneath the cemetery, quickly becoming the town's most celebrated tourist attraction. Later, glass panels were added to protect the mummies from souvenir-seeking visitors who rudely cracked off a finger or toe to take home for show-and-tell.

I had first seen the mummies several years ago on my first visit to Guanajuato. It was in October during the town's annual Cervantes Festival, when after running into one man dressed as Cervantes himself coming out of a bar downtown, and no less than six Don Quixotes and an assortment of Sancho Panzas, I had learned to anticipate almost anything.

But the mummies were something else altogether. They were propped up behind the glass panels as though posing for a bizarre group photo. A mother who had died at childbirth clutched her stillborn baby. Some men wore remnants of suits. Others wore nothing; their clothes had disintegrated while their bodies remained preserved. One woman had on a wedding gown.

But dead is dead. The new exhibit isn't much different from the old, except that the tunnels are now air-conditioned and well lit. Hanging on the walls are framed posters and prints by José Guadalupe Posada, the satirical artist who became famous during the Mexican Revolution for his skeletal caricatures of high political officials. Because it's a Mexican custom to photograph the deceased before burial, photos of the dead are also exhibited.

Some of the bodies are in individual display cases, heads resting comfortably on satin pillows; others are in groups. Some are reclining. Others, with hunched shoulders, hollow eyes, and gaping mouths, are standing or sitting. At least one seems to have just had a haircut, and a tiny fetus is labeled, "The world's smallest mummy."

Guides lead groups of visitors through the displays, lecturing all the while as though at the Prado or the Louvre. I saw one girl of about eleven or twelve years of age staring transfixed at the mummified remains of a young girl perhaps not much older than she. One woman, maybe in her twenties, used the reflective glass of a mummy case to touch up her make-up, watched by the hollow eyes of the occupant inside.

In 1985, the entire mummy collection was sent to Japan, where they proved to be a popular attraction at several museums. The mummies were transported by special jet, with the more fragile of them assigned to first-class seats; the others rode tourist. Fortunately, the airline decided not to sell the remaining empty seats to regular paying passengers. Thus the inevitable was avoided. "Excuse me, sir, is this seat taken? Augghhh!!!"

Along with being a popular tourist attraction, the mummies have a strong community presence. If the local soccer team, the Guanajuato Wasps, have a bad season, disappointed fans dub the players the "Guanajuato Mummies."

The mummies have stirred the creative juices of numerous writers, including Daniel Curley, whose novel *Mummy* (Houghton Mifflin) involves an American who finds his mother's body on display at the mummy museum. He steals it and drives it back to Illinois, stuffed inside a suit of armor propped on top of his Buick. The Mummy Museum is also the setting for the Ray Bradbury classic "Next in Line," included in *The October Country* (Knopf), a collection of his short stories.

The Mexican horror film, *The Mummies of Guanajuato,* filmed on location, has achieved almost a cult following over the years. The popularity of so macabre a display isn't surprising for Mexico, a country where the reality of death is never far from the urgency of life.

"The word 'death' is not pronounced in New York, in Paris, in London, because it burns the lips," Mexican poet Octavio Paz once wrote. "The Mexican, in contrast, is familiar with death, jokes about it, caresses it, sleeps with it, celebrates it; it is one of his favorite toys and his most steadfast love."

While certainly not for the squeamish, and for all of its ghoulish detail, the Mummy Museum in Guanajuato remains in the end a strong, positive statement about the comedy of life.

Morelia

Another colonial city that lives between the present and the past is Morelia, a city often called "The Candy Capital of Mexico." Mexico is known the world over for its colossal sweet tooth, and nowhere are sweets more glorified than here, 185 miles northwest of Mexico City, where the production, sale, distribution, and consumption of candy amounts to a way of life.

Traditional Mexican candy is like no other. It's gooier, sweeter, bolder, with no subtle flavor variations to ponder, no creamy bonbons filled with perfumed centers, no artificial flavors, no preservatives. When a Mexican child is rewarded with a sweet, or *dulce,* most likely it will have the heft of a tortilla filled with beans, and the child's eyes will dance with happy appreciation. Nowhere in the world do eyes express more, say more, than the dark sweet eyes of Mexican children.

Morelia's central plaza, surrounded on three sides by shady arcades and pedestrian malls, is dominated by Morelia's magnificent cathedral, whose twin pink spires guide travelers from miles around to the heart of the city. The cathedral was begun in 1640 and completed 100 years later. It's considered Mexico's best example of plateresque architecture, an ornate style that resembles decorative silver work.

Two blocks west of the plaza, the Mercado de Dulces (the candy market) thrives under the graceful arches of El Clavijero Palace, established in the 1600s as a Jesuit college. Some thirty shops fit neatly into the stone archways, with their displays of sticky delights stacked about in orderly confusion, often seeming to defy all laws of gravity. There's La Casa de las Antes Dulces Regionales next to Húeramo Dulcería, and La Moreliana Dulcería next to Suzy's. Suzy's was closed when I was there. The neighboring shopkeeper said Suzy was out with a toothache.

So as not to gobble up everything in sight, one shops cautiously here. The most famous candy made in Morelia bears the city's name. *Morelianas* are flat caramel-like disks of burnt milk and sugar that are so light and rich that anyone visiting from elsewhere in Mexico is duty-bound to bring boxes of them back for family, friends, and children left behind. Buyers test *morelianas* for freshness by bending them. If they're pliable, they're okay. If they crack or break, they've seen better days. All the stickier candies in the market are wrapped in cellophane, so it's all right to pinch and squeeze them. Attracted by all the sugar, bees are all over everything, but they're so deliriously sated that no one ever seems to get stung. Bees notwithstanding, the market is immaculate.

Ates, the popular jellied-fruit candies that come in a rainbow of colors and flavors and in all forms from solid, brick-shaped packages to bags of assorted gumdrop sizes, were inspired by the region's warm moist climate. Originally, *ates* were a means of preserving local fruits, and they are traditionally eaten with cheese. The recipe, according to one young lady who said she had gotten it from her mother, is to boil three quarts of fruit and one quart of sugar in a copper pot until the mixture is thick enough for you to see the bottom of the pot when the concoction is stirred. Nuns of the early religious orders that helped found the city used to make candies as gifts for the viceroys and bishops and, in doing so, perfected many of the recipes for sweets and confections that are now handed down from one generation of Mexican housewives to the next.

Stacked among the *ates,* the *morelianas,* the sugared pecans, and the lightly dusted chocolate balls are jars of *cajeta,* a caramel sauce made from goat's milk. Part of being a child in Mexico is wearing *cajeta* from ear to ear. Ranging in color from gold to dark brown, it is eaten plain, spread on bread, poured over ice cream, or in more refined circles, used as a sauce for crepes and garnished with walnuts or confectioner's sugar. Also for sale are bottles of light mustard-colored nectar made from eggs and milk, flavored with cinnamon or some other spice of choice, and laced with about 10 percent rum to give it a distinctive flavor. It's called *rompope,* and it's used as a dessert sauce or as an after-dinner drink. My bottle had a picture of Daniel in the lion's den on the label.

At the Dulcería Teto I bought a hockey puck—sized chunk of chocolate flavoring, *chocolate de metate,* that was far too strong for nibbling. Mexico's contribution to the world's list of favorite foods, chocolate originated with the Indians of Mexico and was adopted by the Spaniards when they saw the Aztecs drinking hot chocolate in Moctezuma's court. The cocoa bean, the base from which chocolate is made, was used by the Aztecs as money. Also, the Aztecs believed that chocolate made men who drank it more attractive to women—among other things.

The Mercado de Dulces is open daily from nine to nine, and everything I priced, no matter what it was, seemed to cost about the equivalent of two dollars.

Serious candy devotees might want to step into the Dulcería Atenas at Portal Hidalgo 255, on the north side of the plaza. In this classic candy shop many of the local products are sold along with a variety of European and U.S. candies. Though the wares are fine, if a bit expensive, shopping in this store isn't as much fun as shopping in the candy market.

Several candy factories in Morelia, such as Moreliates at Minzita 50, Jorgito at Gertrudis Bocanegra 1459-A, La Orquídea at J. Jesús Urbina 135, and La Estrella Dorada at J. Jesús Urbina 6 have shops on the premises. While a visit to a candy factory might be less appetizing than it sounds, the shops offer good selections, including elaborate gift packages and baskets.

Morelia acquired its role as the candy capital of Mexico naturally enough. Its lofty altitude and year-round springlike climate encourage the growth of numerous raw ingredients—cocoa (processed into chocolate), coconuts, pecans, sugarcane, guavas, papayas, mangoes, quince, and other exotic fruits. And the lush rolling hills assure good grazing for cows and goats, whose milk is used in many Mexican candies.

Situated 160 miles west of Mexico City on a high plateau and surrounded on three sides by mountains, Morelia is the capital of Michoacán, one of Mexico's loveliest states. The town was founded in 1541 by the royal edict of Antonio de Mendoza, and it quickly became a center for culture and learning. Originally named Valladolid after the city in Spain, its name was changed in 1928 to honor the locally born village priest José María Morelos, who became one of the greatest heroes in Mexico's war of independence from Spain. Today it is an almost perfectly preserved Spanish colonial city.

My favorite hotel here, and one of my favorite hotels anywhere, is the Hotel Villa Montana, perched high up in the Santa María hills overlooking everything in this picturesque colonial city. The Villa Montana was originally to have been the home of actor Tyrone Power and his wife Linda Christian. But Power died of a heart attack before its completion. Now owned by Count Philippe and Countess Eva de Reiset of France, the hilltop Villa Montana is quite literally Morelia's crowning glory.

Soon after Power's death, Villa Montana opened as a seven-room hotel. During the years, cottages, gardens, terraces, and brick walkways have been added, all radiating from the original hacienda-style building. The gradual expansion helps explain the eclectic design scheme in the guest quarters. Each of the seven rooms and thirty-three suites has a different motif, with blue and yellow baths and hand-loomed rugs. All have antique colonial furnishings, broad wooden ceiling beams, or vigas, and cozy fireplaces. (At an altitude of 6,000 feet, Morelia has warm days and nippy nights). On the coffee table in my room were copies of *Antiques, Interiors,* and *Architectural Digest,* all well read and well out of date. One was twenty years old. The cottages—joined with buttressed brick archways and tiled patios—are scattered along terraced landscapes swept by brilliant clusters of bougainvillea. In the spring when the jacaranda trees are in bloom, all the shadows have a purple haze.

Passing through the hotel entryway, guests are greeted by a menagerie of stone-carved animals and figures—saints, gods, fishes, a giant owl, an elephant missing its trunk. Maids wear white blouses and black skirts, with their hair tied in a single braid; even the oldest look like schoolgirls. Some people like to be awakened by church bells or roosters crowing or savage drums. I like the early morning chatter of maids outside my door.

Morelia's duplicity as Old World Spain and New World Mexico didn't escape the notice of Hollywood filmmakers at a time when lush period films were much in vogue. Director Henry King filmed *Captain from Castille,* starring Power, in Morelia for just that reason. Power's costar in the film was an Ohio coed named Jean Peters, who later when she had become an established star, married Howard Hughes.

The bullfight scenes in the movie of Hemingway's *The Sun Also Rises,* also starring Tyrone Power, were filmed in Morelia as well. The similarities between Spain and Morelia are no less striking today.

Managing director Ana Campean runs the Villa Montana with a degree of charm and efficiency rarely found outside the finer hotels of Madrid or Seville. We had lunch together one day, and while her eyes were focused on mine and she listened to everything I said, she signaled a cruising busboy with a simple flick of her wrist, instructing him to clear off an adjoining table. We were talking about art. "Alfredo Zalce lives in Morelia," she said, never missing a beat. "He's one of our country's greatest painters. Maybe I can arrange an introduction."

Even non-guests regularly come for dinner or drinks at the Villa Montana simply to soak up the atmosphere and the spectacular views from the outdoor dining terrace. If the president or some other major VIP is in residence, the hotel may arrange to have the floodlights of the Morelia Cathedral turned on down below for an even more spectacular view.

Tyrone Power would have approved.

Dining at the Villa Montana might be a bit pricey, but savvy travelers can quickly make up for the splurge by eating on the cheap at the Inmaculada, a nightly downtown street fair of sorts sponsored by the Church of the Inmaculada, with outdoor tables and streetside chefs cooking up a storm. Reminiscent of Singapore's famous outdoor "car park" food stalls, it's clean, festive, and fun.

Tables are set up in the courtyard of the church, with cooking stands arranged along the nearby streets. Each stand specializes in something different—tacos, tamales, roast pork, chicken *mole,* steaming soups, chorizo (sausage), and desserts. Tantalizing aromas attract hungry diners from blocks around. The atmosphere is highly social with tables being pushed together and friends joining friends. There's always someone singing or playing a guitar. You can come away well fed for little more than a dollar or two. All proceeds go to the church, which in turn uses the profits to feed the poor.

Despite its easy accessibility, on Highway 15 between Mexico City and Guadalajara, Morelia appears to be seldom visited by U.S. tourists. That's too bad. With its gray and pink stone buildings, sculptured gardens, bubbling fountains, near-perfect climate, Old World ambience, historical sites, and charming candy market, it's truly a treat for the traveler.

Rubén Morales:
Portraits from Morelia's Plaza

*I*never got to meet Alfredo Zalce, but I became good friends with Rubén Morales, long a familiar figure selling his paintings on Sunday at the corner of Zaragoza and Madero, just off Morelia's *zócalo*. Increasingly, he's been winning attention and fans north of the border as well as throughout his native country.

Among a number of galleries now handling his work in the United States is the prestigious Kenneth Raymond Gallery in Boca Raton, Florida, and the Karen Newby Gallery in trendy Tubac, Arizona.

"Almost everyone in my family owns one or two of his works," says Morelia art patron Elsa Medina. "There is something very Oriental about his work, in his bold yet graceful use of lines. All of his figures have large feet. That's very Picasso-esque."

I had purchased a Morales painting several years ago at Morelia's Casa de las Artesanias, where handicrafts from throughout the state of Michoacán are sold on two levels of a 450-year-old former convent located just behind the cathedral. It was a simple painting of a flower vendor that I grew more and more fond of as time went by. Even on the dreariest of days, it seemed to fill the room where it hung with warmth and color. I bought several more paintings on subsequent trips, noting a substantial increase in price each time, although they were still relatively inexpensive at less than $200. But on this visit, none of his paintings were on display. When I asked one of the saleswomen why, she told me they had become too expensive so they weren't handling them any more. "But don't you set the prices?" I asked.

"Sí," she said.

It was quite by accident that I met Rubén Morales shortly afterward. It was Sunday. On the way to El Mercado de Dulces, I passed Las Rosas church and conservatory, now part of the city's art and library complex. On weekends, artists can sell their works outside along the church walls and fountains, and there they were. I recognized Morales' work immediately—faceless figures done in an impressionistic style and heavy, rhythmic swirls of paint applied with brush and pallet knife in the warm bright colors that speak of Morelia's labyrinth of twisting sun-washed streets. Twenty or so of his works were on display, oil paintings as well as drawings and watercolors.

Morales looked like an artist. His facial features were classic Mexican. He had dark curly hair that tumbled over his forehead, dark skin, and a broad swipe of a mustache beneath a somewhat prominent nose. Added to this was the knowing, sensitive look common to those who portray life in the stroke of a brush or pen.

Morales interrupted his chat with two other painters and came over. I introduced myself. I had already picked out a couple of paintings I wanted: a woman with a pail done in a deep blue wash and another of a young woman sitting with her legs drawn up in front of her next to a bowl of orange flowers.

Morales obviously doesn't have far to go to find his subjects. The Las Rosas conservatory is just off Morelia's main plaza. Surrounded on three sides by shady arcades and pedestrian malls, the plaza is dominated by the magnificent Morelia Cathedral. The plaza, like plazas throughout Mexico, is peopled with workers, vendors, and people living their everyday lives. Businessmen gather for coffee at outdoor cafes in the late afternoon, workers sweep the street with palm fronds, old women sell lottery tickets, and kids hawk newspapers and chewing gum. Subjects enough.

When one is seduced by Mexican art, its wealth and accessibility can be almost overwhelming. Two days before I met Morales, I had visited José Luis Cuevas, Mexico's leading contemporary painter.

Cuevas's palacelike, Japanese-style home, with white walls and sliding glass panels, is in the posh San Angel district of Mexico City, not far from the Diego Rivera Studio Museum. The museum is Rivera's former home and workplace that he shared with artist Frida Kahlo just after their marriage in 1929.

I wanted to see Morales's studio and asked if I might visit him there. He said he would get one of the other artists to look after his paintings and I could meet him there at 3:00 that afternoon. He wrote out the address. He lives on Avenida Manuel Buendía, but his studio is about a mile or so in the opposite direction.

Later, as I sat in the taxi on the way to his studio, I looked over the notes I had taken earlier. Morales was born in Morelia in 1947. Son of a construction worker, he was one of a family of five children whose mother had died when he was a year old. He finished elementary school in Morelia and attended art school for two years at the Escuela Popular de Bellas Artes there, but learned little, he says, rebelling against the formal techniques taught at the school. He used to go to the Plaza de Armas in downtown Morelia, where local painters gathered to sell their works. He learned many of his skills as an artist from them. Morales is married to Adela Zarate Alvarado, and they have three grown daughters and an adopted four-year-old son.

Morales was standing at the door as my taxi pulled up in front of the green stuccoed building. The interior of his studio was sparsely furnished with several work tables, geraniums in coffee cans, and a cot, and the back section opened to a cluttered yard where two large pigs snuffled about. Even Salvador Dalí, who loved to shock visitors with his eccentricities, never had pigs in his studio. Part of the studio served as a tailor shop. Morales explained that his wife, Adela, did alterations, nodding to several somber business suits hanging there that were all too large and dowdy to be his. And, of course, paintings were everywhere—drawings, sketches, and oils stacked here and there, on the floor, propped against the walls.

His favorite painter was Diego Rivera, he told me. I asked what he thought of José Luis Cuevas, whose powerful images seem thrust from the subconscious and are often preoccupied with death. "Not much," he said, but his expression acknowledged respect.

I picked out yet another painting—a swirling yellow image of a man stacking melons—and gratefully bought it. Morales cautioned that the paint was still wet.

The next day as I crossed the plaza, I passed the flower vendors sitting on the sidewalk selling their fresh blossoms under the shaded portals. The one in the pink dress, I was sure, was the subject in the painting hanging in my living room at home.

El Rosario: Where Butterflies Are Free

With the first chill of fall, millions of monarch butterflies leave their breeding grounds in the northern United States and Canada and fly unerringly to the fir-covered hills of Michoacán in central Mexico—3,000 miles away. There they thrive in the humid and temperate climate along the mountains that rise above El Rosario. The great clouds of orange and black monarchs, with wings designed like delicate Tiffany glass, attract more than 1.5 million people during the five-month migration period that ends in March.

Many of the area's older residents call the butterflies *"palomas,"* Spanish for "doves" or "pigeons." Others call them "flying flowers."

The hamlet of El Rosario, with several hundred inhabitants, and nearby Angangueo, population 11,000, have benefited greatly from the butterfly phenomenon—improved roads, new mountain trails, stores, and rustic restaurants. Numerous bed-and-breakfast inns and campsites have sprung up, augmenting the Don Bruno Monarca hotel's thirty rooms in Angangueo and the San José Purua's 150 rooms located well outside of town.

Only a few brave souls drive their own cars the final four miles to the butterfly sanctuary. The dusty dirt road is rough, bumpy, and strewn with boulders. Special vans are available to shuttle visitors in and out.

Dancing through shafts of sunlight, many with torn and tattered wings, the orange-golden monarchs are true show-stoppers. They sleep in a semi-trance during the cooler hours and burst forth in a crescendo of color when warmed by the sun.

While seasonal migration is common for birds and bats, such

butterfly migrations are rare, and few of the insects are believed to survive the entire migratory cycle. They reproduce in the warmer states along the way and die, with their offspring carrying on. Each butterfly instinctively begins the migration alone, eventually becoming part of the growing clouds. Those that do make it to Mexico unerringly seek the fir trees (*Abies religiosa*) of Michoacán.

The area's unique neoarctic fir forests are holdovers from the last ice age, and in addition to sheltering the monarchs, they maintain the critical watershed for the entire region. Because of this and the fact that these trees may hold the secret to the spectacular monarch butterfly migration, the Mexican government has declared the butterflies' winter home a nature preserve, preventing logging and further development.

Scientists attribute the monarchs' ability to navigate accurately over such a long distance to biochemical forces that use celestial navigation and polarized rays of the sun. Apparently the insects are somehow programmed to note the sun's position and the time of day, which helps them steer a straight course to their winter home. When researchers at the University of Kansas exposed the butterflies to artificial light, it threw off their internal clock and made them misread their position in relation to the sun.

The monarch butterfly originated 220 million years ago, when Africa and South America were still united as a single continent. Butterflies had great importance in pre-Hispanic Mexico. Their multicolored wings can be seen in the murals of Teotihuacán, carved in stone, or painted in ancient codices.

Numerous myths of life and death concern the butterfly metamorphosis. Warriors frequently wore butterfly images on their chests when going into battle. Romantic poets instilled in them even greater gifts. Because the butterflies come in waves of millions around November 1 and 2 (when Mexico's Day of the Dead is celebrated), many believe that the butterflies represent the spirits of the dead returning.

A bonus for visitors to Angangueo is Casa Parker, the former home of William and Joyce Hartzell Parker, now a museum. The Parkers were British citizens who came to the region in the late

1920s when the area was rich in silver. William Parker was a mechanical engineer who worked for America and Smelting, a British mining firm.

Parker was also a photography buff, and many of his early photos are on display, as well as his darkroom and photography equipment. The house remains as it was, an intimate glimpse of frontier Mexico. Mrs. Parker, a heavy smoker, died of lung cancer in 1975 at the age of seventy-three. Devastated, William Parker, then eighty-five, shot himself.

Francisco Castro Martinez, the Parker's gardener for fourteen years, is the museum's curator. His hours are unpredictable. If he's there, you can pay the small admission fee and tour the museum. Near the Parker House is a restored mining tunnel that visitors may enter. The tunnel ends at the Immaculate Conception Church, built in 1882 and modeled after Notre Dame in Paris. A craft shop across the street from the church offers everything from Christmas tree ornaments to embroidered napkins featuring the butterfly motif.

Mexico City

A flagpole in the central plaza of Aguascalientes, capital of Mexico's smallest state, also named Aguascalientes, designates the exact geographic center of Mexico. It's affectionately called "the belly button of Mexico" by residents of the area.

Aguascalientes may be the belly button of Mexico, but Mexico City is its heart. All skyways, all roadways, all railways—routes in many cases following those laid down by the ancient Aztecs—all dreams and promises, all broken hearts and emotional renewals begin and end there in a city that stands tall amidst sleeping volcanoes and massive mountains rising majestically from the depths of ancient legends. This hemisphere's oldest and largest city is nestled on a lofty plateau that was once the heart of the Aztec Empire, the fabulous city of Tenochtitlán. There is no other city quite like it in the world.

Timed for the year 2000, the city's six-hundred-seventy-fifth anniversary, an extensive $300 million renovation of the city's historic center is currently under way. The Historic Center runs from the Zócalo, as the Plaza de la Constitución or city center is called, to Alameda Park—some 670 blocks in all. The massive face-lift will include the renovation of approximately eighty eighteenth- and nineteenth-century buildings, many of which will be converted into apartment and shopping complexes. A $79-million 400-room hotel will be constructed on the site of the former Hotel del Prado, destroyed in the 1985 earthquake. Two youth hostels are planned near the Zócalo. All are designed to attract residents back to the city's center. At present, many of the restaurants in the area, including several of the city's best—La Casa de las Sirenas (House of Mermaids), the Hostería de Santo Domingo, Los Girasoles—close early in the evening in order to give employees time to get home, because the area isn't particularly safe at night.

The second largest public square in the world, after Moscow's Red Square, the Zócalo has been the site of centuries of human transgression—inquisitions, revolutions, political protests, student uprisings, and demonstrations. Its look was gray and solemn.

The refurbishment of the Zócalo was open to competition, bringing in 250 architectural proposals. One designer suggested turning it into a glass-enclosed solarium. Another envisioned a lake with gondolas.

The winning submission, by architect Ernesto Betancourt, includes a small forest of jacaranda trees, park benches, a fountain, and a grouping of modernistic poles that will incorporate lights, wind chimes, and banners. The entire ground of the Zócalo will be paved with pink marble and stone from Oaxaca. It will also be enlarged by closing off several adjacent streets.

Walking along the Paseo de la Reforma not far from the Bellas Artes, I was approached by two young men. Immediately I bristled, a reflex action learned after years of living in New York with its endless variety of sidewalk entrepreneurs, hawks, and opportunists. But then I felt foolish. These were just kids.

Smiling shyly with the bright white teeth that everyone in Mexico seems to have, they explained what they wanted. For their English class in school, they had to interview a visiting American tourist on a tape recorder—in English—and then play it for their class. No matter how much I like to think that I fit in, a seasoned traveler who walks comfortably between two countries, I can't fool anyone, especially two excited kids with a tape recorder.

"Good morning. What is your name?"

"My name is Ron Butler."

"Ron Boot-lar?"

"Sí."

Uncontrollable giggles followed. *Ron* in Spanish means "rum."

"Where do you live?"

"I live in Tucson. *Tux-son*. Arizona."

"Are you a cowboy?"

"Sí."

The interview continued. How did I like Mexico City? I liked it fine. When it ended, there was a polite smattering of applause from the sizable crowd that had gathered to watch. I think I heard someone mention CNN. Finally, my two young interviewers thanked me. They packed up their tape recorder and headed off in one direction, while I went on in the other. I could have told them that I had been coming to Mexico City almost forever.

I was a student in college when I made my first trip, chasing after the woman I was in love with at the time—the first great rip-your-heart-out love of my life. She was studying Spanish in summer school in Mexico City and had begun dating a young bull-fighter, or so I was informed by a mutual acquaintance. That was all I needed to hear. I couldn't afford to fly to Mexico City, so I took a bus there all the way from Nogales. The trip took three-and-a-half days during which time I ate nothing but the salami sandwiches I had brought with me (I didn't want to take a chance on getting sick). Someone had recommended a cheap hotel, the Hotel Pal, and I checked in there. The bathroom in my room was so small that in order to take a much-needed shower I had to stand with one foot in the toilet.

When I called my girlfriend, she sounded understandably surprised. I could never have found her address without getting lost—she was staying with a Mexican family—so she suggested that we meet at the Sanborn's restaurant in the basement of the Hotel del Prado.

Sanborn's was crowded, but it wasn't difficult to spot her. I had stared into those eyes a thousand times. She was wearing a silk scarf, fashionable then, tied unusually tight around her neck, and she kept nervously adjusting it. At one point the scarf slipped, and peering suspiciously over my cup of coffee, I noticed the bite mark on her neck. Even an incision by Dracula couldn't have been more obvious. A huge row followed, and in the morning I was back on the bus heading north, wishing I hadn't thrown away my few remaining salami sandwiches.

After my interview with the two students and all the walking I'd been doing, I was getting a bit weary. The city's 7,350-foot altitude can quickly tire even the most determined explorer.

I decided to sit for a while on the lower tier of the Juárez Monument at the edge of Alameda Park, only a short walk down the Bellas Artes.

Sitting across from me on the other side of the arena-like Juárez Monument, or "hemicycle" as it's technically called, was a large Mexican family. Like me, they were probably out-of-town visitors who retreated to the park to catch their breath. Brothers and sisters, aunts and uncles, they almost filled the three marble tiers on their side, as though waiting for a show to begin.

The Juárez Monument faces the Reforma, and the wooded green Alameda Park sprawls out gracefully behind it. Only a fraction of the size of Mexico City's famous Chapultepec Park, the largest metropolitan park in the world, Alameda Park was once an Aztec marketplace. Revolutions were sparked there. During the Inquisition, people accused of crimes were hanged or burned alive before crowds of onlookers. Today, Sunday band concerts are held and babies crawl in the grass. Office workers steal into the park for a few moments' reprieve. Men catch up on the newspaper headlines. (The filigree white iron benches could be more comfortable; they were designed at a time when people were smaller.) Nursemaids chase after toddlers who scoot off in all directions. Wooers woo. It's a peaceful, quiet place that has occasionally erupted with political demonstrations and violent protest. Homeless advocates once set up a tent city that remained for weeks in the park. But all was quiet today.

I watched as the traffic light changed and an old man, hunched forward as if walking into an imaginary wind, crossed the Reforma. A little girl climbing on one of the two stone lions that flank the Juárez Monument, said, "Look Mama, I'm not afraid."

Mexico City's principal boulevard, the Paseo de la Reforma was built by the Archduke Maximilian, who in his effort to beautify the city, styled it after the Champs-Élysées in Paris. Originally named Empress Road in honor of Maximilian's wife, Carlota, the new avenue provided more ceremonial pomp and a more convenient route for Maximilian's royal carriages on their daily trip from Chapultepec Castle to the National Palace downtown. It's ironic that the Paseo de la Reforma is now overseen in such stately grandeur by the Juárez Monument. Benito Juárez was the man who ordered Maximilian's execution, and Juárez's extensive land, military, and church reforms were honored by renaming Empress Road.

Juárez, whose likeness can be seen in almost every central plaza throughout the country, was Mexico's only full-blooded Indian president. Born in a small Oaxacan village, the son of Zapotec parents, he is credited with separating church and state. He is often compared to Abraham Lincoln. Both came from humble beginnings, both were known for great personal honesty and political principle, and their contemporary presidencies were each marked by civil war.

A museum devoted to Benito Juárez is located on Avenida Hidalgo near the National Palace. Preserved on the second floor are the rooms where he lived while in office, and where he died in 1872. Official papers, photos, a dressing gown, and even his chamber pot are on display.

A few blocks away from the Benito Juárez Museum, Mexico's tallest building, the Latin American Tower, stands out high above the surrounding city and serves as a directional landmark. Earlier in the day, I had toyed with the idea of visiting its observatory on the forty-second floor, but decided I'd wait for a clearer day.

The sidewalk on the other side of the Reforma resembled a Middle Eastern souk, with peddlers lined up block after block beside sprawling displays of watches, tapes, posters, socks (three pairs for $5), used books, pottery, wind-up toys, T-shirts, neckties, dolls, paper flowers, leather belts, junk jewelry, and just about anything else that might legally be offered for sale. Business was brisk as pedestrians stepped gingerly past the merchandise displays. The street peddlers previously had been restricted to several nearby side streets, but extensive roadway construction forced them to move. And move they constantly do.

Also across the street and a few blocks down is the vacant boarded-up lot where the Hotel del Prado once stood and where a new hotel is being built. The 1985 earthquake caused such massive damage that the Prado had to be demolished, along with many of the memories of my first experience with unrequited love in Mexico.

Surviving the earthquake, however, was Diego Rivera's famous mural, *Dream of a Sunday Afternoon in Alameda Park,* the hotel's prized lobby showpiece and yet another tribute to Mexico City's celebrated park. The artist must have been prophetic when he decided in 1947 to paint the mural on a thin, movable slab of concrete, metal, and stone instead of the solid wall. Thus, it survived the earthquake with only minor cracks. The mural can now be viewed for a nominal charge at the Diego Rivera pavilion, which was specially constructed for its display in Alameda Park not far from the Juárez Monument.

One of the artist's later and best-known works, the fourteen-by-forty-five-foot mural was painted by Rivera a decade before he died. The sprawling fantasy depicts the dreams of two old men who nod off on a park bench. Their visions, in essence, are the political history of Mexico. Rivera himself, shown as a mischievous moon-faced boy with a frog in one pocket and a snake in the other, holding an unopened umbrella, is a central figure in the mural. The artist's second and third wives, Lupe Marin and Frida Kahlo, stand next to him. Kahlo is holding his hand as though more a mother than a wife (a role she frequently played in real life).

Rivera's wit is revealed in such figures as an old war veteran on crutches. Close inspection of the many medals on his chest reveals an empty sardine can. Working with three assistants, Rivera completed the mural in two months and was paid the equivalent $6,000 (U.S. dollars), an impressive sum at the time.

Before I left the park, I glanced up again at the graceful monument of Benito Juárez. The burdens of his four years in office were grave. A great stone angel hovered at his shoulder, and he stared down through the ages in quiet contemplation. The traffic light changed again, and his fellow countrymen, his "children," surged forward in a wall of cars and buses and vans and trucks.

I headed back up the Reforma toward the Latin American Tower for lunch at the Bar L'Opera (Opera Bar). Singing waiters? A dandified setting for patrons of the nearby Bellas Artes stealing away for a nip between acts of *Aida* or *Don Giovanni*? Hardly. The Opera Bar is a cantina. With its gilded baroque ceilings, wrought iron chandeliers transformed from vintage gas fixtures, scrollwork mahogany bar, high-back paneled booths, and red-leather banquettes, however, the Opera Bar is far removed from the swinging-door, spilled-beer-on-the-floor cantina that might come to mind. In fact, it's easily the most opulent cantina in Mexico, a throwback to the Belle Epoque days of President Porfirio Díaz.

When the Mexican Revolution ended, a triumphant Pancho Villa crashed through the door on horseback. The bullet holes can still be seen in the ceiling.

For decades, the Opera Bar remained a bastion of machismo, where meals were light and drinks were heavy. Women weren't allowed in the bar—now the main dining area—but, if properly escorted, they could come in through a side entrance and have dinner in the back room. But since sexual equality was included in the Mexican Constitution some twenty years ago, women have been begrudgingly permitted inside.

When I arrived for lunch at 1:30, I was the only customer. Waiters were fussing about, but none had yet taken a station. All were older and dignified, as are waiters at most of the better Mexican restaurants. Baskets of plump, crisp *bolillos* (rolls) were stacked high on one table, ready to be distributed. The famed scrollwork mahogany bar, looking like something out of the Old West, and surely a mile long, was empty.

I started to sit down at a booth but was motioned to a table instead. The booths were all reserved, I was told. I chose a table close to the door so I could spot a friend who was joining me when she arrived.

Each table is topped with a small red tablecloth placed diagonally over a large white one and each has a bowl of jalapeño peppers festering with onion slices in a thick green juice. Menu specialties include roast beef in its own juice, *cabrito* (roast kid), roast suckling pig, a German plate, and spaghetti *al gusto*.

The roast suckling pig sounded good, but it wasn't; it was a bit too tough and greasy. My friend, who arrived late, had the German plate—knockwurst, mashed potatoes, and sauerkraut—with a beer, which I wished I had ordered instead.

Mexico City is a city you can enjoy even when you're alone, or as alone as you can be with 22 million other people who live within its boundaries and routinely cope with urban and economic ills that could easily devastate any other major city—noise, crowds, pollution, crime, poverty, traffic congestion, political uncertainties, and a lingering monetary crisis. Pot holes that can swallow your car. Taxi drivers who don't know where anything is. Yet, moving at its own snappy tempo, the city flourishes.

Intoxicating aromas waft from the city's fine restaurants. Shops are crowded, hotels full. Museums and art galleries bustle with activity. The city's lofty altitude, combined with its tropical latitude, give it an air of perpetual springtime. Mornings are as light and effervescent as bubbly pink champagne. Well, some mornings at least. Evenings are as lush as velvet.

Daytime temperatures are warm, generally in the seventies. Evenings are dress-up cool. The air pollution you've heard so much about in Mexico City is a little worse in the wintertime. Your eyes may burn, and you won't feel much like jogging along the trails in Chapultepec Park. But there's so much to see and do, you may hardly notice.

Just as Mexican craftsmen can turn the simplest piece of glass, tin, or wood into a charming work of art, so too is the city a showplace of imagination and design.

The city's cultural epicenter is the Zócalo. There one can find the National Palace, with more of Diego Rivera's fine murals. The National Pawn Shop, now as much a museum as a place to seek emergency funds, is located here as well. The nearby Metropolitan Cathedral is a classic example of colonial art and architecture. The massive house of worship was built by the conquistadors with the stones of an Aztec temple that they had demolished.

Over the years the huge cathedral has been slowly sinking into the ground, causing alarm in even the most pious of worshippers. Something had to be done. The combination of a generous outpouring of faith and several modern engineering techniques has kept further descent in check.

Hernán Cortés, conqueror of the Aztecs and depicted as a syphilitic idiot in Diego Rivera's National Palace murals, wins no popularity contests in modern-day Mexico. He is buried in the simple sixteenth-century church of Jesús Nazareno on the corner of Mesones and Pino Suárez, just south of the Zócalo. A plaque on the left side of the altar designates the burial site: Hernán Cortés, 1485–1547. In a country where the spirits of the dead are believed to live in close communion with the living, the tomb's lack of adornment is commentary enough.

Despite the unpopularity of Mexico's conquerors, the Christianity they brought with them took a firm hold. Today, embellished by native exuberance, Christmas in Mexico City is always a colorful highlight. The city is ablaze with lights—more than half a million of them—strung high across the main avenues. Nativity scenes, angels, giant jumping jacks, and huge, gaily wrapped packages decorate parks, traffic circles, lawns, and plazas. The Zócalo dazzles the senses with balloons and crimson poinsettias. Everywhere there are carolers, pastorelas (medieval miracle plays), special Christmas art exhibits, folklore dances, and spectaculars.

Visitors to Mexico City, even those used to snow and sleigh bells, needn't feel homesick at Christmastime. The dazzling street decorations, the lights, the crowded shops, and the people loaded down with packages are all reminiscent of the warmth and traditions of a U.S. Christmas. Most of the churches offer midnight services, the most moving of which is midnight mass at the Metropolitan Cathedral on the Zócalo. The sheer height of the nave adds to the grandeur of the service.

The *posadas* begin on December 16. This series of special fiestas was originally a reenactment of the Holy Family's search for shelter—*posada* means "inn." But now it tends more to reflect the holiday mood of dancing and parties. The final and most important *posada* takes place on Christmas Eve.

Turkey, native to Mexico, is often served at Christmas, but the more traditional dish is codfish and *revoltijo,* a *mole* sauce made with green chiles, and a true delicacy, shrimp patties.

Mexican children once looked to the Three Kings for their toys, distributed on January 6. The Three Kings custom is still widely observed in rural Mexico, but new to an increasing number of homes is the Christmas tree and Santa Claus. There are several nurseries just outside of town where customers can cut their own trees.

And what's Christmas south of the border without a piñata party? Fragile clay pots in fanciful shapes and sizes decorated to re-semble a range of characters—Popeye, whales, elephants, donkeys, Donald Duck, and Snoopy—are filled with candies, cookies, and other goodies and strung aloft. A blindfolded child who has been whirled around and around several times tries to break the piñata with a stick, while the other children at the party try to keep it out of reach by raising and lowering the rope or ribbon to which it's tied. Finally, the stick and the piñata connect. Bang! The piñata breaks, and the goodies spill to the ground. Excited squeals and a mad scramble for candies ensue.

The piñata is one of the many Mexican Christmas traditions that have made their way to the American Southwest. In Tucson, Christ-mas tree ornaments frequently feature strings of chili pepper lights, clay miniatures of old Spanish missions, tiny sombreros, and howl-ing coyotes, along with kachinas and Indian fetishes. Christmas art originally developed as a means to teach the Christmas story to Na-tive Americans. Arched doorways, windows, and wall niches, com-mon to Southwest architecture, lend themselves perfectly to nativity scenes and Christmas displays. And everywhere you look, lumi-narias burn brightly. Tradition has it that the glowing candles in sand-weighted paper bags (the custom derives from the Chinese lanterns the conquistadors brought with them to the new world) light the way for the Holy Family to find a room at the inn.

Public markets and supermarkets in Mexico delight young and old alike with dangling displays of piñatas for sale. Also sold are the many fruits and candies used to fill the piñatas—caramel disks, jellied fruits, gobs of *cajeta,* sweetmeats, sugared pecans, balls of chocolate, tangerines, sugarcane, and quinces.

Rosca de reyes is a ring-shaped cake sold around Christmastime that has a tiny porcelain figure of the Christ child hidden inside. The cake is cut and served on January 6, the Day of the Three Kings. The one whose piece of cake contains the Christ child must host a party on February 2, the day the Nativity crèche is disassembled and put away for the following year.

The Day of the Dead

*E*l Día de Los Muertos, the Day of the Dead, is a combination of Halloween, All Saints Day, and All Souls Day, when it's believed that spirits of the departed return to visit the living. November 1 is set aside for children who have died, November 2 is for adults.

Visitors to Mexico at this time will find *ofrendas,* elaborate altars designed to lure the dead back from the beyond, almost everywhere they go, in shop windows, museums, restaurants, at the popular Bazar Sábado in San Angel, and even in the parks. While most are designed to honor the dead, others have more commercial applications, displaying items for sale to be used for altars at home. Many Mexican families construct these elaborate altars in their homes and cover them with fragrant *zempazuhils,* bright yellow-orange marigold-like flowers, leaving a carpet of petals from their houses to the graves as a "guide" for their loved ones to follow. At night, elaborate bonfires may be built in front of their homes to light the way.

Ofrendas are set up days in advance and may be filled with candied fruits, *pan de muerto* (a sweet, brioche-like bread), tamales, *mole,* tortillas, fruit, books, toys, colored candles, photos of Pancho Villa and Emiliano Zapata, bottles of tequila and mezcal, brightly colored paper and plastic flowers, *calaveras* (papier-mâché skeletons), skeleton puppets, sugar-candy skulls, and perhaps a cigarette or two—anything the deceased may have enjoyed in life.

Along with remembrances and prayers for departed loved ones, the Day of the Dead is also a time for parties and rejoicing, a reunion for living family members, who have come from afar to gather for the occasion, and their deceased relatives and friends, who presumably have traveled even farther. Families visit cemeteries and leave masses of flowers and favorite foods on the graves of the departed.

Anthropologists believe the Day of the Dead to be the oldest surviving celebration in the Americas, with roots deep in Mexico's pre-Columbian civilizations, as a visit to the Aztec Wall of Skulls in Mexico City's Museum of Anthropology will attest. Along with a belief in several afterworlds, the Aztecs also practiced human sacrifice, believing that human blood was needed to sustain the universe. The uniquely Mexican celebration began in pre-Hispanic time as part of the harvest festival. To make it easier to get the natives to accept Christianity, the church let early believers retain some of their pagan celebrations, but shifted the date of the original festival to coincide with All Souls Day.

Most of the Day of the Dead trappings are designed for a one-time use. Others are so exquisitely and masterfully created that they're saved to be used over and over. Some of these end up in museums. The Diego Rivera Studio Museum in San Angel is filled with giant *calaveras,* most of which were created by a single craftsman whom Rivera favored. The Dolores Olmedo Museum in Xochimilco has an entire wing devoted to such figures, one of which unmistakably resembles Olmedo herself wearing a favorite hat. The most famous work of artist José Guadalupe Posada, whose skeletal figures poked fun at high political figures during the time of the Mexican Revolution, is *La Catrina,* which depicts a grinning skull adorned with a nineteenth-century lady's hat. It is recognized throughout Mexico as the personification of death and is seen more than any other figure during Day of the Dead festivities. It appears in full character as the central figure in Diego Rivera's famous mural, *Dream of a Sunday Afternoon in Alameda Park.*

Many of the more tradition-bound communities in Mexico attract thousands of visitors to watch the spectacular Day of the Dead observances. In Oaxaca in the south and Janitzio, the island on Michoacán's Lake Pátzcuaro, all-night candle and torchlight vigils take place at the grave sites. Mixquic, on the southern edge of Mexico City, holds such a traditional celebration.

When Michelle Richmond, a friend and fellow writer who was living in Mexico City, learned of my interest in attending a Day of the Dead celebration in Mixquic she offered to take me.

The Day of the Dead is a national holiday in Mexico, so the Periferico heading south from Mexico City was only moderately clogged with traffic. At a little past 4:00 in the afternoon the November sky was dark and gray. Many of the cars on the highway already had their headlights on.

Our directions were to take the Periferico Sur, exit at Xochimilco, and continue south following the road signs to Mixquic (Mixquic is pronounced like "whiskey" with an m). But of course there were no road signs. Once we left the main highway we drove this way and that, luring anyone we could to the open car window to ask for directions, which were always given with great animation and detail.

Michelle was at the wheel. With us where her daughters Monique and Kimberly, ages twelve and fourteen, two pretty, bright-faced girls who surely must have been a head taller than any of their classmates at school. Both had that wonderful sense of self-possession that young American children raised in a foreign country always seem to have. With two of my own living not far away in Guadalajara, I should know. Could anything, I wondered, be less compelling to two young girls than spending the remainder of the evening and a good part of the night climbing around cemetery gravestones in observance of an ancient ritual in which an entire country is obsessed with death? I had to marvel at their enthusiasm. If it was even the least bit feigned, it didn't show.

"¿Es este el camino a Mixquic?" Michelle yelled past me out the window of the car. A covey of wise men leaned down to window level to point out the way. *"Gracias,"* she said. Continuing on, we soon passed the famous canals of Xochimilco's floating gardens, all lit up at dusk but looking oddly more harsh than pretty that way. We followed a bus for several blocks and, turning with it, finally saw our first "Mixquic" road sign. A collective sigh of relief re-

sounded through the car. The drive was supposed to take forty-five minutes. We had been on the road for nearly two hours. But at least we knew the way now. Driving back would be easier.

I was excited. Mexico's cavalier attitude about death had long fascinated me. During the previous few days in Mexico City, I saw Day of the Dead decorations and *ofrendas* almost everywhere I went.

On the bedside table at my hotel when I arrived was a large candy skull with sunken eyes, gaping mouth, and my name lettered neatly across the forehead. As someone who spends a considerable amount of time in hotels, I'm not unaccustomed to receiving baskets of fruit or an occasional bottle of wine in my room, but this was a first. Traditionally, as I was pleased to learn later on, one repudiates death by eating the candy skull. It wasn't there to scare me away.

We were still several miles from Mixquic when we had to stop to allow a street procession to pass, a group of priests and acolytes leading fifty or so costumed ghouls and ghosts from the cemetery to the church down the block. Church services are held continuously during the Day of the Dead, in essence to welcome the return of spirits who have no living relatives to visit. It passed in almost silent slow motion, and we continued on. Traffic was quite congested now. For all our earlier difficulty, all roads now seemed to lead to Mixquic and we simply followed the flow of traffic, ignoring local entrepreneurs who waved flashlights, trying to direct us to pull into improvised parking lots.

The police-supervised parking areas just outside of Mixquic appeared to be far more reliable. We were motioned to an area on the left side of the road. We pulled in, paid the parking fee, and were then further directed by young men in Day-Glo orange vests to a parking spot. I was impressed. The massive parking operation went more smoothly than those at some of the big football games I'd attended back home. We got out of the car, made mental notes of where we were parked (just east of the big elm and the blue fence), and joined the clusters of people heading along into town on foot. It felt a little as if we were going to Lourdes or Fátima, but there was a sense of festivity in the air. Party time! If the dead were the center of attention tonight, they promised to be lively lot.

Mixquic, with a population of perhaps 19,000, radiates as do most towns in Mexico from its church, which loomed in somber elegance ahead of us, silhouetted against the brown hills and quickly darkening sky. This was no white-washed adobe edifice, as one sees so often in Mexico, but a brooding medieval-looking stone structure that was all but engulfed by the graveyard surrounding it, bridged only by the entrance walkway.

The street as we approached was lined with makeshift stands selling bowls of soup ladled out of bubbling caldrons, tacos, enchiladas, fried pork rinds, hand-carved wooden cooking utensils, vintage movie-star photos, woven baskets, and an endless assortment of Day of the Dead items—offertory candles, *pan de muerto,* frosted cookies shaped like ghosts, papier-mâché skeletons, and the hottest-selling item of all, plastic glow-in-the-dark necklaces supporting a tiny luminous skull. Every child we saw had one, it seemed, or was pleading with harried parents to purchase one.

Closer to the church, the road resembled a carnival midway with more of everything for sale and huge throngs of people milling this way and that. "Stay close. Don't get lost," we kept telling the girls.

The dark sky suddenly opened up, and a heavy shower pelted Mixquic, sending the crowds of people scurrying under the awnings that protected the roadside stands and food stalls. I ended up almost face-to-face with a roasting lamb shank. The crowd became tense when a group of helmeted soldiers bullied its way through, forcing and shoving people out of the way. It sent a shiver through me. "Mi niña, mi niña," a frightened mother called, and someone else scooped up the fallen child. I had seen police who looked like that in Haiti and Beirut—cold, expressionless, harsh. I had never seen them before in Mexico.

The shower didn't last long, and we moved forward to an area where the crowd was thinner. The rain had changed the smell of incense and cooking food from pungent to sweet and musty, and extinguished the candles that had been glowing in the churchyard cemetery. During the day, relatives of the dead had scrubbed the tombstones and lined the graves with flowers and offerings. Groups scattered around us at one grave or another prayed or chanted songs. Others passed one another with a polite though barely audible *"buenas noches."*

When Kimberly, the fourteen-year-old, bent over to read one of the gravestone inscriptions, someone pinched her. Startled, she bolted upright, lost her balance, and was doing a perfect prelude to an arm-swinging swan dive when her mother and I grabbed her. *"Gringa bonita,"* we heard some young boys say with giggles as they disappeared behind a small mausoleum.

We stayed in the cemetery until the air got chilly and our presence seemed like an intrusion. We went into one of the larger and more respectable-looking food concessions, found a table, and ordered some soft drinks, beer, and quesadillas con chorizo, tortillas stuffed with melted cheese and bits of sausage. As we were eating, a slightly tipsy German woman came over from a nearby table and said, "Be careful. They'll try to cheat you here." Sure enough, when our bill came it was about four times more than it should have been, and our subsequent argument with the waiter was loud enough to bring the big, burly manager out from the kitchen to see what was wrong. He looked at the bill, chewed out the waiter, as if he didn't know all along what was going on, and reduced our bill considerably. It was still high, but I paid it. On the Day of the Dead, it's the living you have to watch.

Back out in the thick of the crowd, we passed a fortune teller who worked with a little yellow canary in a wicker cage. The girls urged me to have my fortune told. I gave the man the equivalent of one dollar, and the bird dutifully went to a shelf at the far side of its cage, picked out a folded-up horoscope, and dropped it on the little stand in front of me. The girls squealed with delight and then translated my fortune:

You have had some bad times in the past, but don't be disheartened; many things you desire will be achieved. Various business ventures worry you, but you will soon overcome them and accomplish them. News will arrive soon that will be advantageous to you. Happiness and wealth will follow you in all areas, and without your expecting it, money will be abundant. You will make purchases that will produce great profits. The oracle announces that your life will be a chain of happiness and that you will live for a long time.

How about that? And on the Day of the Dead.

On the way back from Mixquic, just about every house we passed had a bonfire burning in front to help the dead spirits find their way to their relatives' homes.

It was late now, and costumed pranksters were out in force, stopping cars and asking for "contributions." At one point, a vampire slumped over the hood of our slow-moving car, looked up into the windshield, and grinned fiendishly with bloody teeth. We were already rolling up the windows. Further along, a big white coffin in the road opened periodically to allow a glowing skeleton to sit upright. It was clever. We handed some crumpled pesos out the window, and a flesh-and-blood hand quickly retrieved them.

It was nearly 4:00 A.M. when we reached my hotel. Kimberly and Monique were asleep in the back seat of the car. The sun would soon be up, the spirits gone.

Mexican Art

*M*exico City lives, breathes, and personifies art. The first art
museum in the New World opened there in 1781. Invitations
went out, wine was ordered, and a crush of dignitaries, scribes, and
socialites descended on the San Carlos Academy of New Spain of
the Three Noble Arts. Today the city has enough art museums to
keep dedicated gallery-goers soaking their feet in Epsom salts for
days.

Art in Mexico can be traced back to prehistoric times, to the
stelae, temples, and monuments of the Mayan and Aztec Indians.
Take a subway ride in Mexico City, and you'll rumble past Mayan
excavations. No other major city offers such a wealth of art on so
many diverse levels. The Spanish conquistadors brought artists with
them who painstakingly captured the faces and scenes of the New
World while faithfully recalling the saints and passions of the Old.

The revolution of 1910 gave Mexican art a new beginning, and
giants such as Diego Rivera, José Clemente Orozco, and the fiery
David Álfaro Siqueiros rose to paint magnificent murals in broad,
rhythmic motions that spoke in clear poetic and social tones. They
were followed by contemporary masters such as Francisco Toledo,
Carlos Mérida, and Rufino Tamayo. Reflecting a deeply felt na-
tionalism, the murals, which originally served as giant storybooks
for a largely illiterate population, are everywhere in Mexico City.
Murals by the Big Four—Rivera, Orozco, Siqueiros, and Tamayo—
can be found in the Bellas Artes. A massive mural by Rivera adorns
a sweeping stairway at the National Palace; others are on the balcony landing. Across the Zócalo, the National Preparatory School

features numerous murals by various artists; many have been defaced by students over the years because of activist themes. Rivera's first mural is there. The Polyforum Siqueiros, where art is exhibited and performances staged, includes that artist's masterwork, *March of Humanity*. Even the bustling Abelardo Rodríguez Market, located in a working-class neighborhood at Venezuela and Correro Mayor, is filled with colorful murals by such outstanding twentieth-century artists as Pablo O'Higgins, Grace and Marion Greenwood, and Isamu Noguchi.

As an art center, Mexico City excels—find a blank wall, and you'll find an art show. So revered is the painter in Mexico that any artist who can't pay his taxes may pay the equivalent in paintings. The government then hangs them in public places (the paintings, not the artists) for everyone to enjoy. So great is this cache of artwork that the government now has a museum just off the Zócalo (Calle Moneda 4) where more than 3,000 paintings, drawings, and photos are on display. The collection grows by more than 350 pieces per year. The museum is called La Colección Pago en Especie (The In-Kind Payment Collection). Rodolfo Morales, Boris Viskin, Marisa Lara, and even Diego Rivera are some of the artists whose works are on display here.

In no other country in the world do the sun and the moon play such symbolic roles in the lives of its people, from the human sacrifices of the past in exchange for favors granted by these celestial orbs to the clay sun faces decorating today's homes and the moon medallion dangling from a small girl's neck. Mexico glories in its Mexican-ness, its *mexicanidad*. Fiery heroes of the Mexican Revolution are as venerated as *madre e hijo,* mother and child. The sun and the moon also play strong roles in Mexican art. Huitzilopochtli, the Aztec god of the sun, was venerated as the source of light. Author Octavio Paz speaks frequently of the mask of the Mexican face in his best-known work *The Labyrinth of Solitude*. Two major archeological sites located twenty-three miles northeast of the city are the Temple of the Moon and the Temple of the Sun. During nightly sound-and-light performances, the voices of Vincent Price, Charlton Heston, and Burt Lancaster, among others, help bring Mexico's legendary past vividly to life, so I'm told. As many times as I've been here, the sound system has never been in working order. Tamayo frequently repeated the sun and the moon theme in his work. Wrote Octavio Paz, "If one could say in a single word what it is that distinguishes Tamayo from other painters of our time, I would say, without hesitation: sun. It is in all his paintings, visible and invisible. Night itself, for him, is nothing other than the sun seared black."

In no other place in the world (except perhaps Florence, Italy, where variations of Botticelli's *Venus* can be found peeking into every jewelry store window along the banks of the Arno) do people visiting museums so closely resemble the artwork they come to see. In the spectacular Museum of Anthropology in Chapultepec Park their faces are reflected in the figures on display, from fiercely arrogant warriors of the Middle Mochica Period to the shy, winsome Jalisco figures with large heads and comically elongated noses. Suspended in time, these images transcend the ages, conveying moments of joy, sorrow, fear, pride, contemplation, and surprise. Even erotic figures, often boldly explicit, possess a naive charm.

There are bowls and vessels of every imaginable kind, from utilitarian household wares to classic Mayan works that rival anything created by the early Greeks. Clay dogs, ducks, whistles, gold pendants, textiles, and stone carvings, all speak of a rich and imaginative past. Experts contend that you can tell whether a pre-Columbian work is genuine by picking it up. If it feels right, chances are it's real. Dip it in water, and you can smell the earth from which it was made. Touch your lips to it. If they stick momentarily, it's real. If they don't, it's not. Sounds silly, but it's true. But don't plan on taking anything but reproductions home with you. Tough cultural heritage laws established more than two decades ago make it illegal to transfer out of the country pre-Columbian, colonial, and certain major works of art by leading painters. Deliberate infractions can result in stiff fines and imprisonment. It's all a far cry from years ago, when every souvenir shop in Mexico displayed baskets of pre-Columbian figures and shards that shoppers carted off at bargain prices. Even today in Guatemala, pre-Columbian jade and ceramic figures found by peasants in the fields are often used to reinforce building cement.

In a city filled with museums, one of my favorites is one of its newest, Museo José Luis Cuevas, located in the former Convent of Saint Ines in the city's center. With its high walls and a beautiful central patio, the convent blends well with the historic palaces and narrow streets all around it. The museum follows the trend in Mexico of artist-patron museums, where a private museum showcases an artist's personal art collection along with generous samples of his own work. (The Tamayo Museum, the Diego Rivera Museum, and the Frida Kahlo Museum are others.) Cuevas is considered the leading artist in Mexico today, or at least the leading artist in the so-called "breakaway period" (the departure from muralism). His powerful images seem thrust from the subconscious and often show a preoccupation with death. (He had a long, near-fatal illness in the mid-1970s.) Particularly impressive is the towering abstract sculpture, *La Giganta,* in the museum courtyard, dwarfing everything in sight. The front view is female, the rear view is male. An outstanding collection of Picasso prints is also on display, as well as a collection of erotic engravings by Cuevas (scenes from actual bordellos and cabarets). Born in 1934, Cuevas enjoyed early success as an artist. He had his first one-man show in Mexico City at the age of nineteen.

Another favorite museum is the Museo Franz Mayer, located in a former Spanish colonial hospital on the Plaza de Santa Cruz and facing two historic churches. The German-born philanthropist's stunning collection is described as "marvelous everythings" by my New York friend Jean McGrail, who tipped me off about this place. The treasures include rugs, furnishings, silver, paintings, and tapestries, more than 8,000 pieces in all, plus more than 20,000 antique ceramic tiles. Among the outstanding pieces is *St. James the Moor-Killer,* a two-foot-high eighteenth century gilded and polychromed wooden statue, trimmed with leather, iron, and hair. Mayer, known as Don Pancho to his friends, was a dapper man who always wore a carnation in his lapel. He lived in Mexico from 1905 until his death in 1975, and he willed his fabulous collection to the city in gratitude for the fortune he amassed there. At night the Plaza de Santa Cruz is gloriously flood-lit.

Along with its wealth of art museums and public murals, Mexico City also has an impressive number of private galleries. Galería de Arte Mexicana, established in 1935, is one of the country's oldest and most prestigious galleries. (It staged Frida Kahlo's first Mexico exhibit in 1953.) Galería de Arte Misrachi, located at Genoa 20 in the San Miguel Chapultepec area of Mexico City, is also well regarded, offering the works of such famous painters as Rufino Tamayo, José Luis Cuevas, and Francisco Zuniga. Warm and bookish Hardy's at Genoa 2 in the Zona Rosa has a good selection of contemporary paintings and bronzes. If I were planning a career as an art thief (and I'm sure several gallery owners have suspected that I might be casing their gallery with just such intentions, I've been back so often), I'd head first for anything by Rivera or Tamayo, artists whose styles couldn't be further apart but who speak much the same language. Photographs of the Mexican Revolution by pioneering photographer Agustín Victor Casasola and *calaveras* by José Guadalupe Posada, the short, chubby, mustachioed printmaker whose work spoke out so satirically during the Revolution, would also fill my robber's satchel. And surely there would be a place under my jacket somewhere for a bronze sculpture by Humberto Peraza, best known for his monumental works of bulls and matadors that grace plazas and avenues in many Mexican cities as well as the bullrings in Juárez and Tijuana. Peraza created his first sculpture at the age of five (he's now nearly seventy) and has produced 6,000 pieces since. Even today, he rushes home after a bullfight to recapture the dramatic moments in clay to be used later as models for large bronzes.

Despite the reverence shown to its rich heritage, much of Mexico's modern culture reflects that of its neighbor to the north. Julia Roberts, Brooke Shields, Clint Eastwood, and other U.S. film stars are idolized, along with baseball's Fernando Valenzuela. *Sesame Street* and the *Smurfs* are the top television programs for kids. *Archie, Dennis the Menace,* and *Superman* dominate the comic book market. And bosomy, blue-eyed blondes stare seductively from billboard advertisements.

Cuernavaca

Sidewalk cafes along the *zócalo* are jammed. Traffic stops. Horns honk. Families in their Sunday best stroll—playing both observer and observed. It is a typical weekend on the *zócalo* of Cuernavaca.

Cuernavaca's *zócalo* is one of the most spirited of all in a country that marks every leisure hour with a celebration, as though there might never be another. The sound of marches emanates from a colossal bandstand in the middle of the square. Balloon and trinket salesmen hawk their wares. A toddler poses for photos, propped precariously astride a brightly painted wooden horse while parents coo just beyond camera range. The white-haired photographer pokes his silver head in and out from beneath the camera hood. Click! Sigh of relief. The frightened baby is lifted down. The scenario is repeated as another apprehensive beribboned youngster is lifted into place.

With its red-tiled roofs, clay steeples, and pastel-colored buildings, Cuernavaca is the quintessence of small-town Mexico. Residents of Mexico City, and visitors like myself, weary of the capital's jackhammer pace, flee here for peace. Numerous artists and authors have also sought sanctuary in Cuernavaca. Until his death in 1992, artist Rufino Tamayo lived and worked here, as did David Álfaro Siqueiros, whose workshop and studio at 2 Calle Venus in the Jardines de Cuernavaca district is open to the public.

Octavio Paz, the 1990 Nobel laureate for literature, was another local resident. Several years ago, the famed Mexican poet and author gave a poetry reading at New York's 92nd Street YMCA, long known for its distinguished lecture series. I was there with a copy of his *The Labyrinth of Solitude,* considered the definitive book on life and thought in modern Mexico. As soon as the program was over, I went rushing backstage to have him sign it and found myself herded into a group of his relatives and friends. I must have looked as though I belonged, because as we left the backstage area, walking together, he had his arm around my shoulders. I didn't realize there was a planned reception afterwards where he would be signing books. By the time the reception ended, I had three inscribed books. The following year Octavio Paz won the Nobel Prize for Literature. He died in 1998.

Emiliano Zapata was another well-known local figure. The fiery hero of the Mexican Revolution grew up in a village near Cuernavaca called Anenecuilco. At the age of thirty, with a motley band of peasants and Indians, he sacked and burned every hacienda in the state, reclaiming the land of his people.

Photos of Zapata, with his piercing eyes and flowing mustache, are everywhere—in Harry's Bar and Tabasco Charlie's, in paintings and murals, and in the windows of corner *tiendas.* The main road into Cuernavaca is called Avenida Zapata. The rider of the equestrian statue galloping in place through the center of the town's main traffic circle? Emiliano Zapata.

More recently, Malcolm Lowry's brilliant book *Under the Volcano* was set in Cuernavaca (the novel uses its original name, Quauhnahuac) as was John Huston's stylish film version starring Albert Finney and Jacqueline Bisset. The events of the Joycian novel unwind in the course of a single Day of the Dead celebration.

The rich and the famous were coming to Cuernavaca when Acapulco was little more than a boat landing. They spend their winters basking in its dappled sunlight and stroll in its well-kept gardens amid bursts of red and purple flowers.

Cuernavaca is awash in brilliant flowers that thrive on its high altitude and subtropical climate. Mexico's famous Christmas flower, the poinsettia, originated here. It's named after Dr. Joel Roberts Poinsett, the American ambassador to Mexico from 1825 to 1829. He discovered the flower while on a diplomatic mission to Cuernavaca and brought samples back to raise on his South Carolina estate.

The poinsettia came to be, according to Mexican legend, when a young peasant boy was praying at the altar of his village church on Christmas Eve. In his prayers he apologized that he had no money to buy the Christ child a present for his birthday. In response to his prayers, the first Christmas flower blossomed at his feet. Poinsettias have adorned Christmas altars ever since.

The history of Cuernavaca reflects the history of Mexico. In pre-Conquest Mexico, Aztec Indians came to Cuernavaca to bathe in its warm mineral springs. Maximilian and Carlota dallied there after becoming emperor and empress of Mexico at the behest of Napoleon in what surely must have been the happiest days of their tragic lives. (She went insane following his execution. Vain to the end, Maximilian gave each member of his firing squad a gold coin and asked that they not shoot him in the face.) The restored royal Borda Garden with its pools and shaded walkways is now open to the public. Some say Maximilian and Carlota still meet there, embrace, and then vanish into the past.

Just off the southeast corner of the *zócalo* is the Palace of Cortés, built in 1530. As a reward for having captured the country, Cortés was offered any part of Mexico as his own by the King of Spain. Cortés chose Cuernavaca.

Long the legislative seat of the state of Morelos, the Palace of Cortés is now a museum. Its prized possession is a mural by Diego Rivera, commissioned in 1930 by Dwight Morrow, U.S. ambassador to Mexico at the time (and father-in-law of Charles Lindbergh). Rivera brought his young bride Frida Kahlo with him while he worked on the murals. The expanded honeymoon was probably the happiest time in their tempestuous relationship.

Cortés also founded Cuernavaca's magnificent Cathedral of San Francisco in 1529, one of first churches in Mexico to be built on the massive, sober scale of European cathedrals. Eleven o'clock Mass on Sunday morning lightens things up a bit with singing mariachis.

After Mass, lunch at the nearby Las Mañanitas restaurant is all but mandatory. It's quite literally Mexico's best restaurant. White and green peacocks, flamingos, and African crested cranes saunter through a brilliant sprawl of gardens filled with life-sized Francisco Zuniga bronzes of pear-shaped Mexican ladies. The outdoor dining terrace melds gracefully into the garden, where heavily limbed trees bend gently onto the green sloping lawn and a frantic busboy can occasionally be seen racing out to separate two peacocks squabbling over the attention of a rather plain-looking peahen.

The sculptures have been a fixture at the restaurant since it opened some forty years ago. Since then, both the artwork and the kitchen have grown with success. Zuniga's work is prized throughout the world. Las Mañanitas's frozen chocolate black bottom pie is no less renowned.

Listed on a blackboard menu and served on large blue and white plates, Mexican specialties include steaming green-corn tamales, chiles *rellenos* (mild chiles stuffed with cheese, fried in batter, and served with an onion-flavored cheese sauce), and *carne asada,* a broiled steak fillet rubbed in olive oil and served with frijoles, tomato, and guacamole that comes in its own wooden bowl. After dessert—the pie, of course—there's coffee and a complimentary creamed Kahlua.

Las Mañanitas, named after the popular Mexican birthday song, is owned by Rubén Serda who greets presidents and locals alike with unflappable cool.

Once a private hacienda, Las Mañanitas also has a twenty-three–room hotel complex arranged around a pool and an interior courtyard, but its rooms are booked so far in advance that you almost have to know the owner to get in.

Another notable hotel in Cuernavaca, about fifteen minutes south of town, is Sumiya, the former home of Woolworth heiress Barbara Hutton. The upscale Camino Real chain opened Sumiya as a hotel in 1994, incorporating it into a modern 170-room lodge that retains much of the estate's original oriental furniture, sculpture, and artwork.

The hotel's layout comprises a graceful cluster of four-story buildings connected by a roofed corridor. Its green leafy gardens, fountains, and picturesque walkways, with sweeping views of distant mountains, are reminiscent of a Japanese painting. Hutton is said to have selected the site because snow-capped Popocatépctl, a dormant volcano visible in the distance, reminded her of Japan's Fujiyama. She even had peasants working in the adjacent fields dressed as coolies.

Hutton purchased the property in 1957 and, with Hawaiian architect Albert Ely Ives, spared no expense in creating a Japanese-style palace that she called Sumiya, "House on the Corner."

It was inspired by an early courtesan's home she had seen in Kyoto. She filled the house with priceless antiques, Oriental screens, silks, indoor rock gardens, and imperial furniture. Outside were flower-decked moats, bridges, pools, temple carvings, and fountains. A Kabuki-style theater, where dancers and musicians from Japan performed, seated forty. It's still used for ceremonial functions and meetings. The main bedroom of the house is now the hotel dining room.

Hutton married Raymond Doan at Sumiya on April 7, 1964. Her seventh and final husband, Doan may or may not have been a Laotian prince. Hutton had a penchant for titles. She had previously married two princes and a count. She also exchanged marriage vows with Cary Grant and Porfino Rubirosa. As with most of her marriages, her final union was short-lived.

In 1976, with her health deteriorating and her financial resources shaky, Hutton sold the $3.5-million Sumiya to a Mexican lawyer for a mere $500,000. It was turned into a restaurant before being acquired by the Camino Real chain.

Dubbed "poor little rich girl," Hutton died in 1979 at the age of sixty-six.

From Cuernavaca two great volcanoes can be seen off in the distance, Popocatépetl and Ixtacihuatl, known as Popo and Ixta for short. According to Aztec legend, so great was the love of a prince and a princess who had lived thousands of years ago that a god turned them into mountains so that they would never be separated.

Oaxaca: On the Trail of D. H. Lawrence

The thirty-six–room Hotel Francia, near the main plaza, is clean, neat, and freshly painted. Yet it's not on the tourist beat. Most guide books don't even list it.

But on a quiet Sunday morning I went there on a quest. I wanted to see the room where famed British author D. H. Lawrence stayed while in Oaxaca.

The city of Oaxaca, capital of the state of the same name, is 250 miles south of Mexico City. Of all the cities in Mexico, Oaxaca, with its moody air of intrigue and its large Indian population, is my favorite. D. H. Lawrence must have felt the same way. The author of *Sons and Lovers, The Rainbow, Lady Chatterly's Lover,* and a score of other literary classics and his German wife, Frieda, arrived in Oaxaca on November 9, 1924, after a brief stay in Mexico City. They came by train, transferring from the Oaxaca train station to the hotel on a trolley pulled by two mules.

Lawrence had come to North America initially at the behest of heiress Mabel Dodge Luhan, who lived in Taos, New Mexico. The Lawrences stayed in Taos about twenty-two months between 1922 and 1925. Lawrence, who was suffering from the early stages of consumption, spent his winters in Mexico because of its mild weather.

On his first trip to Mexico, he stayed at Lake Chapala on the outskirts of Guadalajara, where he wrote the first draft of *The Plumed Serpent,* a novel set in Mexico.

On his second trip, he decided to go to Oaxaca because, as he wrote to a friend, "Lake Chapala has not really the spirit of Mexico, it is too tamed, too touristy."

Had Lawrence lived to see Lake Chapala today (he died in 1930 at the age of forty-four in a sanitarium in Italy), he would have been mortified. The town has the largest population of American expatriates in Mexico. The lake is a major water source for rapidly expanding Guadalajara. So much water has been drained from the lake that nature can no longer replenish it. Lake Chapala now has less than one-third of the water it held in 1923, when Lawrence described it as a great "expanse of water, like a sea, trembling, trembling, trembling to a far distance." Its average depth is nine feet. The lakeside yacht club is now so far away from the water's edge that boat owners have to take a taxi to get there.

Traveling to Oaxaca with Lawrence and Frieda (who was six years his senior and daughter of Baron Friedrich von Richthofen) was their friend and frequent travel companion, Lady Dorothy Brett (then forty-one, daughter of Viscount Esher). Surely, little of the trio's celebrated status was apparent when they arrived at the Hotel Francia at 7:00 that night by mule-drawn trolley.

Most travelers to Oaxaca today opt for such upscale hotels as the Camino Real, a beautifully restored 1576 convent; the Victoria, located on a hill overlooking the city; or the Misión de los Angeles, a lushly gardened resort-style hotel ten blocks from the center of town.

But in 1924, the Hotel Francia, named after its original French owner, was the place to be. Built as a single-story hotel in the 1890s, it was so popular that a two-story annex was later added. The room rate when the Lawrences arrived was four pesos a night, with the peso at the time being worth about fifty cents.

When I arrived at the hotel, the young lady at the reception desk, who also handled the hotel switchboard, was having a spirited phone conversation with a friend. She stopped talking for a moment to see what I wanted. I told her I was interested in D. H. Lawrence, and she immediately summoned an aging bellman and instructed him to take me to room 140. Then she went back to the phone.

The room where Lawrence and Frieda stayed is on the second floor overlooking the lobby (in 1924, an open patio). The room, once described as "spacious," was rather small. It hadn't been made up yet; its twin beds were a tangle of sheets. The floor was tiled. There was a mirror and a desk. The toilet seat in the bathroom was white plastic. (Odd, what stays in your mind.)

The Lawrences later rented a house from the Reverend Edward A. Rickers, a local priest, but returned often to the hotel, where Lady Brett kept a room looking onto the street in the single-story section. The rented house was at Avenida Pino Suárez 43 (now No. 600). When it was rattled by a minor earthquake, the Lawrences were quick to move back to the hotel. The house, on one of the city's main north-south boulevards, has since been remodeled into apartments, and no apparent trace remains of the Lawrences' brief stay there.

During his nearly six months in Oaxaca, Lawrence rewrote *The Plumed Serpent* (originally titled *Quetzalcoatl*) and major sections of *Mornings in Mexico,* the title of which is something of a misnomer. While the collection of essays deals with a number of Oaxaca experiences—Market Day, a visit to Huayapa, and such—its main focus is on Indian ceremonials in and around Taos, New Mexico.

Then as now, the city of Oaxaca boasts the largest Indian population—about 90 percent—of any Mexican city. The Lawrences must have surely stood out. The slightly stooped, red-bearded British author was irascible and withdrawn. He was invariably accompanied by his doting, full-bodied German wife who had limp blonde hair that no doubt suffered in the Oaxacan humidity. Also at his side was Lady Brett, who was all but deaf and carried an ear trumpet and an electric hearing aid as large as a briefcase at all times.

Lady Brett was one of the first of the liberated ladies. She was a talented artist as well as a gifted photographer and writer. It is largely through her efforts that Lawrence's twenty-two months in Taos and his trips to Mexico have been so meticulously chronicled. However, her attention to Lawrence, or vice versa, began to get on Frieda's nerves, and after a terrible row, Lady Brett left Oaxaca and returned to Taos.

Oaxaca has grown sixfold since the time of Lawrence's visit. Yet, in a way that is unique to Mexico, much of the past remains in place.

The huge central market that Lawrence writes about so eloquently in *Mornings in Mexico* is only a block from the Hotel Francia. The cathedral, the *zócalo,* the Mixtec ruins of Mitla, and its large open-air crafts market that the Lawrences visited are all unchanged.

As much as I admire the memory of D. H. Lawrence, my favorite hotel in Oaxaca remains the Camino Real. Declared an international landmark by the United Nations Educational, Scientific, and Cultural Organization (UNESCO), it's housed in the sixteenth-century Convent of Santa Clara and has been long been considered one of Mexico's true hotel gems.

Until recently, however, sampling this elegant taste of history required more reservations than the kind you make at the front desk. The hotel furniture was clunky, draperies were heavy, and the rather smallish rooms were more or less unventilated. It was a convent, after all.

But thanks to a $1.6-million restoration, guests now truly feel close to heaven. New bathrooms, air-conditioning throughout, all-new furnishings, sound-proof windows. All ninety-one rooms have been renovated.

The Camino Real is built around a series of flowered courtyards, one with a heated swimming pool. Another, with a large stone basin at its center and covered with stone arches, is still called *"la lavandería"*—the laundry. It's where the nuns washed their sheets, habits, and linens. Today, it's a popular setting for weddings.

I sat in the window of my room there one night, in the shadows with the lights out, watching a wedding and the champagne reception afterwards. The little orchestra played "Luna azul" (Blue Moon), the one song if any that Gerta and I had shared. Surely the gods were taunting me. Later, I tried to call Guadalajara. I wanted to talk to the children. But there was no answer.

The property is dotted with 400-year-old frescos, archways, gardens, and fountains. Antique furnishings, colonial art, and colorful regional handicrafts fill the public rooms. My kind of place.

With its large Indian population, Oaxaca is the center of trade for the surrounding villages. On Saturdays, Indian women spread out blankets at the Benito Juárez Market, displaying shawls, cloth puppets, wooden combs, and woven bags. Nearly every imaginable article used in everyday life is sold here.

Oaxaca, once a sacred site of the Zapotec Indians, offers several archaeological treasures. Monte Albán, only nine miles south of the city, with its famous Temple of the Dancers, is one the best preserved of the pre-Columbian ruins. Numerous organized tours with English-speaking guides are available through local travel agencies and hotels.

Mitla, about twelve miles from Oaxaca, offers buildings that resemble Greek-style geometric designs, with walls of inlaid stone mosaic. Nearby is the famous Tule tree, an enormous cypress believed to be more than 2,000 years old. It stands 140 feet high and has a trunk diameter of 138 feet. The tree dwarfs a nearby colonial church.

Two of the country's best-known figures were from Oaxaca, president Benito Juárez and artist Rufino Tamayo. Juárez's birthplace is open to the public, and the Tamayo Museum, displaying the artist's spectacular collection of pre-Columbian art and artifacts, is a city highlight. Art buffs might also want to track down the studio of Oaxaca's Francisco Toledo, one of Mexico's greatest contemporary painters. The studio of Rodolfo Morales is located in the nearby village of Ocotlán

Art takes on a whole new meaning during Oaxaca's Fiesta de los Rábanos (Festival of the Radishes). On December 23, the town's predominantly Indian population turns the *zócalo* into a carved-radish art gallery. Radishes in all shapes and sizes are crafted into Nativity scenes, figures of saints and animals, flowers, churches, and other imaginative designs. The ornate vegetables are exhibited on tables and stands, with prizes going to the most original. Radishes were a great gourmet delight during the Spanish colonial days, and the Radish Festival emerged from the elaborate table displays of the period. As with all Mexican fiestas, music, colorful costumes, fireworks, and dancing are all part of the fun.

Christmas Eve in Oaxaca is equally memorable. Candlelight processions march slowly from many churches and eventually converge on the *zócalo,* where the evening evolves into more singing, dancing, and fireworks.

Shopping Notes

*O*axaca offers a rich variety of Native handicrafts displayed at street corner stalls and in sprawling markets throughout the city. Prices at the source are always lower than retail outlets, so the savvy shopper will find the best bargains and selections by visiting the villages on the outskirts of Oaxaca. Rarely have I left Oaxaca without being loaded down with bags and boxes—and on occasion a newly purchased suitcase—filled with handicrafts and gifts. My philosophy is simple. If it's not worth schleping home, it's not worth having. And I was always buying presents for the kids.

Oaxaca's stunning black pottery is made in San Bartolo Coyotepec. On Route 175, the village is well marked and is served by local buses. The black pottery has a satiny sheen, often with a silvery luster, obtained by burnishing the clay with a piece of quartz before firing. Shaped into tiny pots, animal figurines, beads, bowls, candelabra, jars, jugs, and platters, the black pottery is perhaps the most distinctive of all of Oaxaca's handicrafts. The pottery is sold in private yards and in multi-stalled buildings beside the road.

Alebrijes, animals carved from copal wood and painted with surrealistic designs in vivid colors, are made in the villages of Arrazola and San Martín Ticajete, about fifteen and thirty minutes southwest of Oaxaca, respectively. Shoppers go from house to house visiting each carver's showroom to pick out their favorite pieces, some of which seem thrust from their creator's worst nightmares. Highly prized and expensive when purchased outside of Oaxaca, *alebrijes* are so inexpensive here that they seem like giveaways. All, that is, except the work of Arrazola's master carver, Manuel Jimenez, who was the first to create the wooden fantasies. His prices range from $300 to $1,000 or more. Appropriately, his house is the only one in the village with air-conditioning, a cable satellite dish on the roof, and a Mercedes in the driveway.

Fine cotton textiles colored with natural dyes are made in Santo Tomás Jalieza, south of Oaxaca. Women work on small looms in the center of town, weaving elaborate belts, table runners, and wall hangings. The brightly colored belts, called *fajas,* are sold in bundles throughout the state. The distinct pink color comes from the tiny black cochineal bug found in the white, spongy, weblike substance that clings to the nopal cactus (a species of prickly pear). In a process used by the early Zapotecs, the bugs are boiled down, dried, and then soaked in water into which the color emerges.

Traditional green-glazed plates, bowls, cups, and figures can be found in Atzompa, located on the outskirts of Monte Albán. Tuesday is market day, but a door-to-door search at any other time will generally prove fruitful. *Cerámicas* is the operative word. Green-glazed figures of musicians—violin-playing goats, flute-playing deer, and pigs tapping away on drums—are a special find.

On Fridays, the region's largest weekly market is held in Ocotlán de Morelos, forty minutes south of Oaxaca. Wood carvings, embroidery, cotton textiles, ceramics, woven baskets, and sharp, well-sheathed cutlery attract enthusiastic shoppers. The town's recently restored colonial church is a photographer's dream.

Veracruz: City of Music

S ad, sentimental love songs waft over the *zócalo*. With its
European-style outdoor cafes and strolling marimba bands, the
zócalo in Veracruz is one of the most animated in all of Mexico. But
on Tuesday, Friday, and Saturday evenings, it moves to an even
more bewitching beat as the Plaza de Armas (as the square is officially called) gives way to the ritual of *danzón*. That's when Por-
teños (natives of Veracruz) of all ages, dressed to the nines, demon-
strate their natural rhythm and grace on the cobblestoned square,
worn smooth by centuries of dancers. *Danzón's* origins, deeply
rooted in the bolero's soulful magic, are Cuban. The highly stylized
dance combines elements of the fox-trot, rumba, mambo, and
tango. It is always performed to live music.

Many of the dance couples met for the first time here and fell in
love; others come together briefly in a courtly, sophisticated embrace, without conversation and with facial expressions as fixed as
Mayan statues. Direct eye contact, even by husband and wife, is as
inexcusable as stomping on your partner's feet.

No less stoic are the faces of the musicians, cheeks puffed and
brows gleaming. They wear traditional short-sleeved, white guayabera shirts—both the climate and culture are tropical. Nearby are
rows of chairs and benches for spectators who gather to watch, or
for dancers who need a brief reprieve. It's the place to see and be
seen. During the dance numbers, abrupt musical pauses give the
dancers time to catch their breath, adjust their clothing, or scan the
crowd for a familiar face. Then, just as suddenly, the music begins
again.

To preserve the *danzón* tradition, a Veracruz dance academy run by Lorena Lira Rivera offers nightly classes. Many young men, who clearly would rather be bullfighters, are dragged kicking and screaming to the school by their mothers. But after weeks of lessons, they emerge with new-found social graces. "And it's a good way to meet chicks," one of them confided to me in Spanish.

The music of Veracruz, Mexico's largest port and first European settlement, is a fusion of African, Caribbean, and Latin sounds. It's where "La Bamba" originated, the tune that swept the world when musician Ritchie Valens grafted it to a rock-and-roll rhythm. But nothing quite touches the soul more than the music and magic of *danzón*.

Agustín Lara

*B*efore Selena, before Enrique Iglésias, before Luis Miguel, there was Agustín Lara.

La Casita Blanca, the magnificent two-story home on Avila Camacho Boulevard, Veracruz's waterfront drive where the famous composer, singer, and musician lived, is now a museum devoted to his life and work. Lara (who wrote such songs as "You Belong to My Heart," "Granada," and "María Bonita") was born in Mexico City but long considered Veracruz, "that little corner where the waves of the sea make their nest," his true home.

La Casita Blanca, now the Agustín Lara Museum, was presented as a gift to the legendary composer by the governor of Veracruz. It has marble floors throughout, and the upstairs living room and balcony look out onto the harbor. A white C. Bechstein piano with yellowed keys and a white satin settee flanked by a silver champagne bucket reveal Lara's elegant lifestyle.

Lara was known as the "Irving Berlin of Mexico," less for the mood of his music—mostly melancholy love songs—than for his output and popularity. Like Berlin, he could neither read nor write music. He tapped out his tunes on a piano and let others set them down on paper. He wrote more than 600 songs in his long and prolific career.

Displayed throughout the house are wall after wall of photos taken in night clubs, bullrings, and radio and movie studios with celebrities, beautiful women, famous singers, band leaders, and presidents. Also shown are billboards, magazine covers, letters, paintings, programs, and musical scores. A desk in the bedroom contains eighteen leather-bound volumes of news clippings.

Lara's music pours from wall speakers, on this day the romantic bolero, "Solamente una vez," was playing. Almost daily, Rodolfo Escalante, a talented local pianist and Lara devotee, drops in to play a few of the maestro's tunes.

The upstairs area also includes a replica of the xew radio station from where Lara's nightly *Blue Hour* mesmerized Mexican audiences for nearly two decades. All of the great singers of the day appeared on the program—Pedro Vargas, Jorge Negrete, Pedro Infante, and the Águila Sisters.

Blue was Lara's signature color. When he played at the Capri, the Jacaranda, or any of the other popular night spots in Mexico City, his show invariably opened in a midnight-blue–lit room. Blue also described his demeanor as the slim, gray-haired, sad-looking Lara walked to his piano, accompanied by the music of an unseen trumpet and violin. Then, from the darkness, the violin section would emerge, moving through the audience as Lara's music filled the room.

Slight of build, the five-foot-ten Lara at his most robust weighed only 110 pounds. One of his snappy linen suits is displayed in a glass case near the museum's upper stairway, attesting to his slender stature.

A framed cartoon on an upstairs wall depicts Lara with a little dog looking up at him. "Don't you think I'm a little too bony for you?" reads the caption.

A bronze statue of Lara by renowned Mexican sculptor Humberto Peraza graces Avila Camacho Boulevard. A small replica of the statue can be seen at the Café de Portal, Veracruz's best-known coffeehouse restaurant. As a young, struggling artist, Peraza received a letter from Agustín Lara, who had just seen one of his exhibits and was impressed enough to write, "I would like someday to have your hands sculpt my hands." Peraza never met Lara, but it was a poignant stroke of fate that in 1975, after the composer's death, he would be commissioned to create a statue in his honor. Copies of the statue can be seen in Madrid, Mexico City, and Los Angeles. A framed copy of Lara's letter still hangs in Peraza's Coyoacán studio.

A piano prodigy, Lara left home at sixteen during the final years of the Mexican Revolution to ride with Pancho Villa. Later he was a professional baseball player and even tried his hand at bullfighting.

But always he was most at home performing in smoky bars and brothels. One night while he was playing, a deranged beauty named Yolanda pulled a knife from the garter under her skirt and slashed his face from mouth to ear, then fell at his feet begging forgiveness.

This gaunt, sad-eyed, scar-faced wisp of a man went on to become one of the great sex symbols in Mexico, something of a cross between Humphrey Bogart and Valentino. He was frequently mobbed by women in the streets.

At the peak of his career, he divorced his actress-wife, Carmen, to romance the beautiful rising film-star María Felix, whom he married in 1946. He lavished her with all the spoils of his success— diamonds, minks, Cadillacs. She left him the following year, and he was heartbroken.

The resulting "María bonita," one of his top hits, was written for her. ("Remember those nights in Acapulco, María of my soul?") María Felix went on to become a legendary screen goddess. One of the framed color photographs in the house shows Lara sitting on the floor with the beautiful young María Felix draped over him and hugging a large stuffed dog. He always loved her, though he married three more times. Lara died in 1970.

The Agustín Lara Museum brings the visitor into the glamorous and somewhat sad world of the charismatic composer whose words and music touched the soul of Mexico. On Avila Camacho Boulevard, immediately adjacent to the popular La Mansión Restaurant, the museum is open Tuesday through Sunday. Lara records, tapes, and books are sold in the reception area.

Coffee Break

I like a good cup of cappuccino in the morning, a procedure of coffee-making that in my house takes on ritualistic overtones.

I grind the beans (only the finest Mexican beans, of course). I have a froth-making machine, separate from the cappuccino machine, that makes huge, billowy puffs of milky foam. My Mexican lady friends tell me you have to put the foam into the cup first and then add the coffee. I'm not at all sure why, but I do it. Then I add about a half a shot of *rompope,* a Mexican dessert sauce that comes in various flavors (vanilla is the best for coffee). Finally, I add a dusting of cinnamon. (You can actually tell your fortune by how the cinnamon settles on top of the foam, but we don't have time for that now.) If you do it quickly, before the ingredients begin to settle, the steam works its way up through the foam, the *rompope,* and the cinnamon. It's one great cup of coffee.

By this time, my kitchen is a total mess. There are coffee beans on the floor, foam all over the place, coffee stains on the counter and on the walls. But it's worth it. I've been negotiating for some time now to buy one of those big antique coffee grinders, the kind found in old mercantile stores out here in the West, but so far my efforts have been unsuccessful. It would take up what little room I have left in the kitchen, but what the heck. For a good cup of coffee I can always find another house.

Of course when I travel, I take my quest for a good cup of coffee with me. The world's best cup of coffee, aside from what I whip up at home, can be found right here in Veracruz at the Café de Portales.

I've had coffee in Brazil, in Costa Rica, in Colombia, on the Kona Coast, and on the Ivory Coast. None compares.

I've sat cross-legged on a pillow in Istanbul, where the coffee beans were roasted, pulverized, and brewed in front of me and the finished product was served only when the creamy foam on top, *kaimaik,* signaled perfection. It doesn't come close.

I've visited the coffeehouses of Greenwich Village, where each cup came with equal servings of Kerouac and Baudelaire. Disappointing. Vienna coffeehouses, so pretentious and dainty, are for sissies.

There is nothing particularly imposing about the Café de Portales (formerly the Café de la Parroquia; a family squabble led to the name change) at Independencia 1187. It's long and low, with florescent lighting, ceiling fans, off-white walls, and round, white Formica-topped tables. If a bus or two were parked out front, you'd think you had just wandered into a bus terminal cafeteria.

It's early morning, and this is no bus terminal. The place is packed. Businessmen reading newspapers. Students. Off-duty cab drivers. A pair of transvestites whose five-o'clock shadows are showing through their make-up. A guy selling Cuban cigars works the room. (Veracruz is a major seaport and Mexico's gateway to Cuba.) Another plays violin, his glassy eyes recalling some distant, far-away recital.

Near the front entrance, a marimba band is performing. If the musicians look a bit sleepy, it's because they've been up all night playing from table to table for tips at the outdoor cafes that line the nearby Plaza de Armas.

Waiters in white shirts and dark trousers scurry about taking and delivering breakfast orders, while others carry kettles of boiled milk in one hand and coffee in the other. Patrons signal their need for a refill by tapping their spoon against their glass. The waiters pour several inches of coffee, actually the essence of coffee—boiled-down to a deep, dark richness—into the glass, filling the rest with hot milk. They pour from a considerable distance. Amazingly, the hot liquids arc into the glass and not all over the customers.

It's simply the best coffee ever. If it tastes a bit sweet, it's not sugar, it's the milk (no doubt from contented cows). The glass is hot. You'll need a napkin to hold it. I don't know why the coffee is served in glasses instead of cups. Depending on who you ask, glass is preferred to cups because it's less corruptive to the coffee taste, it holds heat better, or the company simply got a good deal on glasses. A child's first taste of coffee, as was mine, is apt to be the little bit his mother pours into his glass of milk to warm it. It's all very Freudian.

At the far end of the cafe is a pair of great gleaming silver coffee urns manned by a gap-toothed gentleman who could be firing up a locomotive or a calliope. The manufacturer's brass nameplate reads: Latorino Express, Super Macchina, Tokino, Italia, 1884.

The Gran Café de la Parroquia was founded in 1823 and was converted into a cafeteria in 1927. *Parroquia* means "parish." Social life in those days revolved around the church, as it still does in many parts of Mexico. The Cathedral of Veracruz is right across the street, and church officials with traditionally demanding tastes—it was the Capuchin monks who gave us cappuccino—still stop in.

So successful was the cafe that a second one opened some years ago along the waterfront at Insurgentes Veracruz 34 and is named after the original Café de la Parroquia. It seems to draw a younger crowd who, along with their coffee, like to order "flying saucers"— a ham, cheese, and turkey sandwich on French bread flattened into the shape of a Frisbee. In fact, the night I was there some revelers— or maybe they were fighting—sent one flying across the room.

The state of Veracruz is the main coffee-producing region in Mexico. (The state of Chiapas to the south is another major coffee producer.) Veracruz and the towns of Córdoba and Coatepec form the industry's "golden triangle." Leading coffee growers are clearly the lords of the land. Eighty-seven-year-old Juan Martinez Ruiz, who founded Cafes Coatepec, one of the area's most successful companies, still shows up daily to help his son Juan Martinez, who now owns the firm, get things done.

The tropical coffee plants thrive in the region's hot, moist climate and 4,500-foot elevation. So lush is the region that it's often called "Mexico's Garden of Eden." In this giant hothouse atmosphere, plants frequently sprout from bird droppings on tree branches and telegraph lines. Bananas, whose broad leaves shade the coffee plants, are so plentiful that farmers routinely feed them to livestock.

The coffee is sold everywhere—in storefronts, shops, and even from sidewalks where local entrepreneurs scoop the beans from 100-pound gunnysacks to sell to waiting lines of rebozo-clad housewives. The better shops feature coffee liqueurs, souvenir knick-knacks made from the wood of the coffee trees, and one-kilo (two-and-a-half–pound) packages of coffee in little burlap sacks.

In addition to coffee, Mexico's fiery hot jalapeño pepper is a product of the region. They're named after Jalapa, the state capital of Veracruz.

(If Córdoba, Coatepec, and Jalapa, all look a bit familiar, it's because the Colombian scenes in Harrison Ford's movie *Clear and Present Danger* were shot there.)

Coffee plants need constant attention. Because the blossom and both the green and the ripe fruit (called the coffee "cherry," with two beans inside each one) all occur at the same time, harvesting must be done by hand. Despite such labor-intensive production, coffee prices are low. On my last visit to the Café de Portales the prices (figuring about fifteen cents per peso) were reasonable: espresso or American coffee, four pesos; small *lechero* (coffee with milk), four pesos; large *lechero*, six pesos; cappuccino, eight pesos. The house breakfast—a potato omelet in turkey broth garnished with sliced jalapeño and onion—was fifteen pesos.

Excellent coffee is available throughout Mexico. A particular treat is café de olla, coffee made with brown loaf sugar, with cinnamon and cloves added for taste. Known as ranch-style coffee, it's traditionally served in little clay mugs (ollas). Often, coffee producers add sugar to green coffee beans during the roasting process, giving the beans a deep dark sheen and a hint of caramel flavoring.

Places by the Sea

*A*capulco. Ixtapa. Zihuatanejo. Puerto Vallarta. The names read like poetry. Glittering jewels in the 2,000-mile stretch of perpetual summer that winds its way along Mexico's Pacific coast, they conjure up images of showy sunsets; long, loping strands of beach; hillsides carpeted with pale and purple orchids and forests of guava, bamboo, and bananas; that first tangy shock of a frosty margarita touching lips already touched by the sun. Mazatlán. Guaymas. Puerto Peñasco.

Called the Costa de Oro (the Gold Coast), the Mexican Riviera is all palm-frond green and scented with fragrance. Spanish explorers reached this coast by way of the Sierra Madres, making their way arduously by horseback or on foot. Today's visitors arrive in silver jets at modern airports laced with enough cool, gray marble to build another Acropolis. They come by air-conditioned cars and buses and by luxury cruise ships to enjoy the sultry caress of the tropics. The bank clerk shedding his business suit, the account executive from Chicago, the actress—"Didn't she win an Oscar for *Shakespeare in Love?*"

Playa Blanca's Club Med

I'm not fond of organized fun. Theme parks and cruise-ship social directors always send me running the other way. But Club
Med villages in Mexico seemed to be proliferating—the haughty
French vacation resorts have apparently blended well with Mexico's casual, carefree mañana mood. I decided to check one out.

Midway between Manzanillo to the south and Puerto Vallarta to
the north, Playa Blanca on the Costa Careyes is one of the earlier
and most popular of Mexico's Club Med resorts. The French do
marvelous things with sun, much the way they do marvelous things
with food. Nobody blisters, nobody peels, nobody wears hideous
white sun gook on the nose. Both men and women have deep,
breath-taking golden-cocoa tans and waists the size of napkin
rings. No wonder it was the French who created the bikini.

My charter flight from Mexico City, an extension of a Sunday
morning flight from Los Angeles, had hardly landed at the Manzanillo Airport when we were assigned rooms and roommates
(part of the get-acquainted fun at Club Med is that everyone traveling alone has to double up). We then boarded buses that would take
us to the club, an hour's drive away. Over the weekend, other
groups from the Midwest, New York, and Canada were met in
similar fashion, ready to begin their week in the sun.

Clutching my camera, hand baggage, and room assignment slip,
I had the distinct feeling as we pulled away that I was going off to
summer camp. An older woman—a lady of seasoned vintage—sat
next to me.

As soon as we settled into the lull of the drive, she leaned over and said, *sotto voce,* "How would you like to go swimming in the nude?" I didn't know what to say. Was she taking a survey or making a pass? I babbled something in Spanish, and perhaps assuming I didn't speak English, she got up and changed her seat.

Actually, while nude bathing is quietly tolerated at many Club Meds around the world, it's strictly forbidden in Mexico. As we were to learn during our first day's orientation, anybody who wanted to risk an all-over tan would lose it fast enough in a dark Mexican jail.

The village (once you get there, Club Meds are always called "the village") was laid-back attractive, sprawling up the side of a cliff in a network of Mediterranean-style bungalows, all awash in brilliant clusters of bougainvillea. It had all the usual Club Med amenities—beach, pool, central restaurant, bar and entertainment complex, tennis, scuba diving, snorkeling, sailing, yoga, body massages, and poppet beads for money. I bought a new string of beads each time mine ran out, and by the end of the week, I twirled them about with reckless abandon as I headed each night toward the sound of the music at the fountain of eternal spring.

My roommate turned out to be a pleasant enough fellow from Providence, Rhode Island, who had never been to Mexico before and was somewhat apprehensive. He even washed out his socks and underwear in bottled water.

It's generally understood at Club Meds that once you've settled in, you can make your own roommate arrangements, male or female, everybody willing. But according to the law of natural selection, mine anyway, anyone willing to play house on such short notice was probably worth avoiding. Besides what would I do with my friend from Rhode Island? And his laundry?

Opportunities for more gradually developed relationships did present themselves—sunlight is a natural aphrodisiac. But my room was so high up the side of the mountain that, even if I did lure anybody up all those stairs, I'd probably be breathing too hard to do anything about it.

The Chef de Village (the club's managing director) was Greg Russell, an Iowan, who at the time was the only American Chef de

Village in the entire Club Med system. Twenty-eight or so, tall, trim, with free-range hair sculpted high by wind and humidity, he had all the women at the club after him. I was invited to a cocktail party at his lair one night, where I admired his collection of large pre-Columbian statues. I picked one up, explaining to a few of the guests that you could tell if a piece was genuine by the way it feels, at which point the piece I was holding disintegrated in my hands, shattering into dozens of pieces.

"Obviously not real," I said sheepishly. Fortunately our host, who was quite gracious about the whole thing, agreed, saying that it was a reproduction and had been repaired several times before. I was relieved, but couldn't help but notice that the next time he had a party, no invitation was slipped under my door.

Acapulco

*D*ay begins in Acapulco when the sun splashes everything with color—igniting greens and fiery purples between the blue bay and the pink clouds. No matter how late you go to bed, you'll always wake up with that first brilliant touch of day.

In one of the top floor suites of a seaside hotel, the sudden rush of light wakes a tall, tawny-haired blonde, who gets out of bed in a single movement, a graceful tangle of long and well-tanned arms and legs. Because her balcony is one that assures privacy, she pads outside wearing nothing but a good night's sleep. Then she lets out a shriek.

Swooshing past her balcony is a man dangling like a Raggedy Ann doll from the harness of a huge red-and-white–striped parachute pulled by a rope attached to a speedboat. The man smiles broadly. The woman runs inside.

It's been rumored that Acapulco has lost its position as the queen of Mexican resorts. It's so staid now that it even has a Wal-Mart. Cancún is more fashionable, say the travel mavens. Or Puerto Vallarta or Ixtapa or Zihuatanejo. But don't you believe it.

The big Wal-Mart in Acapulco is right on the main drag, Costera Miguel Alemán, named after the late flamboyant Mexican president who headed the Ministry of Tourism when his presidential reign expired. Alemán is credited with turning Acapulco into the mega-world-class resort it is today. If the sight of an Acapulco Wal-Mart, where the ultimate in chic is a haircut at its Unisex barbershop, isn't shattering enough to your sense of place, there's a just-opened Hooter's across the street.

But rest assured, Acapulco is not only hot—it's sizzling.

The ancient Babylon of North American resorts, Acapulco got its start as a major tourist destination during the early days of World War II. The threat of German U-boats off the eastern coast of the United States forced wealthy vacationers to find new places to play.

It was once said that you had to be a millionaire to enjoy Acapulco, but that's no longer the case. The playground for millionaires has long since become the playground for millions. Yet having a dollar or two in your jeans never hurts.

The local gentry live more or less exclusive private lives tucked away in the stately villas that line the palm-groved nooks and crannies of the Las Brisas hills. Their homes sit at the end of long, winding roads or hang off the sides of cliffs. That's so nobody can find them.

The elegant villas all look pretty much alike—open and airy with Spanish arches, broad patios and terraces, doorways without doors, windows without glass. All face away from the afternoon sun, a cooling factor that allows sunsets to be observed in quiet meditation and genuine awe from the dining terrace at margarita time.

Among Acapulco's many splendid sites is the fifteen-story Acapulco Princess, shaped like an Aztec pyramid, with two adjoining towers added since its opening more than two decades ago. Howard Hughes spent his last days sequestered there in such privacy that whenever the maids came to clean he was wheeled into another suite.

Next door to the Princess is the Hotel Pierre Marqués. It was originally owned by John Paul Getty, who spent all of his days somewhere else. He never even laid eyes on the property. Tarzan movies used to be made out back.

Acapulco offers much to see and do amid the glitter—jungle hunts, bullfights, city bus tours, Fort San Diego (a restored eighteenth-century Spanish fortress, now a museum and occasionally the site for fancy open-air parties), an amusement park, fishing, boat tours, and swimming with dolphins at Cici Aquatic Park. Yachts such as the *Fiesta* and *Aca Tiki,* with pirates in costume marauding about the deck, cutlass in hand, offer cruises around the harbor, with drinks, dinner, and non-stop music included.

Acapulco's newest splash is the Shotover Jet boat rides through the jungle canyons of the Papagayo River, about forty-five minutes north of the city. Due to their unique propulsion system, the jet boats hit speeds of forty miles per hour and can turn 360 degrees in an instant, sending a cascading wall of water all over the boat's twelve to sixteen occupants. It's something akin to a roller-coaster ride combined with white-water rafting helmed by a kamikaze pilot. Life vests are mandatory, and there are lockers ashore to store cameras and other valuables so that they don't get wet.

The first of their kind in North America, the Shotover Jet boat rides are an import from New Zealand. They are named after the Shotover Canyon, where the thrill rides were first offered. Five boats are currently in operation.

If you prefer your action in a slightly more passive manner, the best place to watch the famous La Quebrada cliff divers is from the promenade across from the gorge, where crowds begin to gather hours before each performance. (The divers plunge twice daily, at 12:30 noon and again at 10:30 P.M.) A more comfortable, but more expensive, vantage point is the tiered dining terraces of the La Perla nightclub, located in a hotel adjacent to the cliffs.

The 150-foot dive, a feat comparable to diving from the roof of a fifteen-story building, is made even more perilous by the slope of the cliffs. A diver has to propel himself out far enough to clear the masses of jagged rocks on the way down. Split-second timing is required because the inlet below is only twelve feet deep. A successful dive can only be made into the full swell of the incoming surge. There's no charge for watching, but afterward the dripping-wet diver comes by to pass the hat.

Twenty-eight divers, ages seventeen to thirty-four, participate in the ritual, alternating in groups of seven to ten each day. Originally, one large family took part, passing the art on to maturing youngsters; but now outsiders are also accepted into the elite, now-unionized group. Native boys first began the sport by daring one another to dive off ever-higher points on the cliff.

So much of what Acapulco is today is due, at least in part, to what it was before. Although new hotels seem to be going up in Acapulco every day, the recently renovated hillside sweep of white stuccoed, tile-roofed villas known as the Villa Vera remains a symbol of the past; of its dashing owner, band leader Teddy Stauffer, who was married to Hedy Lamarr; and of an Acapulco drenched in wealth and decadence. Even today, no guest speaks to another without being properly introduced. Brigitte Bardot and Gunther Sachs were married there. So were Liz Taylor and Mike Todd.

Mention romantic hotels anywhere and Las Brisas comes instantly to mind. The hotel begins along a spectacular sweep of white sand beach and then climbs lazily up the Las Brisas hillside in a honeycomb of 300 pink and white bungalows. Terraces are surrounded by tangles of tropical color, and just about every room has its own secluded outdoor pool. Las Brisas was made for love.

In matters of dress, Acapulco is one of those fashionable places where millionaires dress like peasants and peasants try to look like millionaires. Anything goes, as long as it's chic, casual, and an off-shade of white. At night, short sleeves for men is as gauche as wearing socks.

As a regular visitor to Acapulco since the days when you could sleep on the beach and not get hassled, I view Acapulco's constantly changing and ever-expanding face as a mixed blessing. I'm excited for its progress, but saddened by its losses.

Puerto Vallarta

*A*ficionados consider Puerto Vallarta, unspoiled by the recent sweep of development that has changed so much of Mexico's traditional tempo and appearance, to be the purest of its popular resorts.

And by far the most exotic.

A favorite location of Hollywood filmmakers, Puerto Vallarta frequently serves as the sultry backdrop for mysteries and romances alike.

John Huston's film *Night of the Iguana* has generally been credited with putting Puerto Vallarta on the map. La Jolla de Mismaloya, the spectacular all-suite resort hotel and convention center, was built on the isolated peninsula of Mismaloya, where the film was shot. Recently, the Night of the Iguana Set Restaurant (Noche de la Iguana) opened in the set that served as Maxine Faulk's (Ava Gardner) hotel in the film. Photographic stills showing the stars in action on the site (part of a collection belonging to the Museum of Modern Art Museum in New York City) are on display along with photos of Puerto Vallarta in days gone by. It also features film clips of the making of the movie. Huston's former home at Mismaloya serves as one of the more casual of the resort's seven restaurants. Through his films, *The Treasure of the Sierra Madre, Under the Volcano,* and *Night of the Iguana,* the director created a relentlessly beautiful tapestry of Mexico, even at its seamiest.

Ava Gardner cavorting with brown-skinned beach boys, Richard Burton and Liz Taylor scandalizing everybody by having an affair while both were married to someone else, Huston pouring another

Herradura tequila—all wove a kind of forbidden magic, a scintillating decadence that remains today.

Indeed, it's part Hollywood legend and part history that makes Puerto Vallarta more than just another pretty string of beaches and discos. Pirates and explorers came to Puerto Vallarta as early as the 1500s; later, Sir Francis Drake and treasure ships from the Orient came. Now instead of treasure ships, the beaches are lined with popular nightspots like Christine's, Carlos O'Brien's, and Friday Lopez. Although such clubs can be found in most of the tourist resorts, the fact that they're located beachside in the shadow of legends makes them that much more appealing.

The city's main focal point is the Church of the Virgin of Guadalupe. The ornate crown on its steeple, Puerto Vallarta's best-known landmark, is a replica of the one worn by the Virgin of Guadalupe in the Mexico City basilica. Local wags sacreligiously compare it to the Corona beer logo, also a crown.

Framed by mountains and fast-shifting cloud masses, Puerto Vallarta's latitude is precisely that of Hawaii's. In the lush outlying foothills, terraced gardens suggest Bali. Everywhere, the air is heavy with a faded sense of intrigue and mystery.

Swiss-born Chris Schlittler, former general manager of the Fiesta America, one of Puerto Vallarta's two premier hotels (the other is the Krystal Vallarta), spent three years as managing director of the Holiday Inn in Tibet before being assigned to Puerto Vallarta. He finds an odd, almost mystical similarity between the two places, particularly in the unhurried gentleness of the people.

The same naïveté is evident in the work of Puerto Vallarta's best-known painter, the late Manuel Lepe. He won international fame through his whimsical paintings of Puerto Vallarta children. Hundreds of little round-faced boys and girls, angels mostly, people his work. They pilot planes, climb trees, drive buses and bakery trucks, float in the air, or peek happily out of windows at the world.

Lepe himself was born into a family of twelve children, so it was only natural that he was drawn to them as subjects of his art. "Look around you," the self-taught artist would say, "Puerto Vallarta is filled with children. They are everywhere, and they are beautiful."

Lepe was born in Puerto Vallarta in 1936. He began painting at a young age, the only child in his large family so artistically inclined. He received his first major commission, to paint a mural for an American couple, Marguerita and Henry Wood of St. Paul, Minnesota, at the age of fourteen. He was a painter for the rest of his life.

Lepe's formal education ceased at grade four, and his artistic skills were self-taught. As with many primitive painters, he simply couldn't tolerate empty spaces on his canvases. Blank skies and broad backgrounds were filled with fantasy, bright colors, flowers, trees, and happy angels. Though naive and self-taught as a painter, he was astute at public relations. Fidel Castro has a Lepe painting hanging in his Havana home. Former presidents López Portillo and Luis Echeverría and Queen Elizabeth of England also own his work, as did the late Richard Nixon. The paintings were presented as gifts from the Mexican government at state presentations for visiting heads of state.

Mexico's Department of Tourism has featured Lepe paintings in a number of international promotions. One widely distributed poster shows yellow-thatched and red-tiled rooftops, with sailboats bobbing in the sea beyond. "The next place to heaven," reads the poster, "a place of untouched charm and beauty."

Lepe's oil paintings cost thousands of dollars, but his work is widely distributed in affordable prints, silk-screen posters, and lithographs. Several fashion lines include decorative embroidery of Lepe scenes on dresses and skirts.

Lepe's work hit a strong progressive stride during the last few years of his life. His show of 125 paintings, acrylics, and serigraphs at the Los Angeles Museum of Science and Industry was viewed by more than one million visitors during its three-month run. He was commissioned to do a large mural in the Municipal City Hall, and UNICEF (United Nations Children's Fund) selected his *El arbol de Navidad* (The Christmas Tree) as a greeting card, which particularly pleased him.

The large mural inside the Municipal City Hall near the bay was his last work. Lepe began the mural in 1982, but it was completed by another artist when death claimed the talented painter in 1983. He was forty-six.

When Elizabeth Taylor and Richard Burton purchased their home in Puerto Vallarta (now a thriving bed-and-breakfast inn called Casa Kimberly), the previous owner had twenty-four Lepe paintings on the walls. As part of the sales agreement, the Burtons insisted that the paintings remain. In less happy times, after their marriage had failed twice, the house was frequently leased or loaned out to friends and several of the paintings disappeared.

"They couldn't have been very good friends," reflected Lepe. "Not if they stole the paintings right off the walls."

Located in the state of Jalisco, Puerto Vallarta was named after Ignacio Luis Vallarta, governor of the state in 1918 when the town became a municipality. It's situated in the curve of a perfectly formed bay called Bahía de Banderas, the Bay of Flags.

The first thing visitors see when they arrive at the airport in Puerto Vallarta is a sign: *Bienvenidos a este alegre lugar,* it says. Welcome to this happy place.

Long-time visitors are inevitably surprised. The more Puerto Vallarta grows, the more it stays the same. The once-drowsy seaside village now has a population of nearly 250,000. It's hardly a village anymore.

Yet donkey carts still clip-clop along cobblestoned roads. Many downtown streets are still unpaved. Women wash their clothes as they've done forever, on the banks of the Río Cuale, drying them on flat stones in the shade of hastily erected palm-thatched ramadas.

By law, all homes must be painted white. Most are topped with red clay–tiled roofs. Even the local supermarket, Gigante, has a cobblestoned parking lot to preserve the primitive flavor of the seaside jungle setting. All the cobblestones come from local riverbeds. Everywhere, brilliant clusters of bougainvillea tumble over patio walls and along hotel walkways.

In the late afternoon, a few of the local gentry still meet downtown over a cup of good dark Mexican coffee or an icy bottle of Carta Blanca beer in the lobby lounge of the Oceanic Hotel, one of the oldest in town. At one time it was the place where everyone in town came to collect messages or pick up mail. The old bar in the Oceanic has been converted into a hot spot called Tequila's. Nearby, a traffic light, designed in the shape of a small lighthouse that used to blink stop and go, stands abandoned on the side of the road. Cars traveling along the waterfront drive rarely paid much attention to it anyway.

Hemmed in by thickly forested mountains, Puerto Vallarta's urge to develop inland is kept in check. Instead, it sprawls up and down the coast, resulting in a well-defined downtown area and two distinct residential districts. The classy, so-called "Gringo Gulch" section of town along the Cuale River has been usurped in recent years by a more prestigious enclave known as Platinum Bend. Sotheby's International Realty, part of the famed New York and London fine arts auction house, handled the sale of one home here that was listed at just a tad under $3 million. The ad carried an Equal Housing Opportunity notation.

The sea horse is Puerto Vallarta's official symbol. The large sculpture of a sea horse on the *malecón* was a 1960s gift from the governor. The nearby dolphin sculpture was a gift from the town's classy sister city, Santa Barbara, California.

Never far away anywhere in Puerto Vallarta is a beach, with the ocean drawn in close and cool sea breezes moving across the land. As at coastal resorts everywhere, it is the temperament of the sea that sets the tone of each day.

Ixtapa and Zihuatanejo

Zihuatanejo, about 150 miles up the coast from Acapulco, was once the quintessential sleepy little fishing village. After settling in, few visitors ever wanted to leave again, it was so pretty. The village had a South Seas look about it—scratchy phonograph music came from thatch-roofed restaurants along the bay. Big-beaked birds squawked out from the jungle brush, and the roar of the surf on the white-sand beach was relentless, each loud crash followed by moments of silence.

Sportfishermen came on the track of marlin and sailfish. Boats with fresh oysters arrived around ten in the morning. A cold beer and a dozen oysters, served up with a little lemon juice and tabasco sauce, was the local breakfast of champions. Palm trees swayed in the breeze, gently rocking the hammocks stretched between them. Footprints in the sand dissolved in the water's rhythmic wash. Only an old, washboard road and a dirt airstrip linked Zihuatanejo to the rest of the world. It was the ideal escape from Acapulco when the music and the smiles began to grate on the nerves and the margaritas tasted warm and watery.

Then Ixtapa came along. A government-conceived FONATUR (Fondo Nacional de Fomento al Tourismo) project, it's one of those computer-designed resorts that Mexico turns out with cookie-cutter precision. Ixtapa was built from scratch, like Cancún and Huatulco Bay. Bulldozers carved out the infrastructures. Major highways were developed along with an international airport, a water purification and treatment facility, and dozens of hotels and restaurants, shopping complexes, discos, and dives. A new marina and yacht club have added to the glitz.

The Camino Real hotel alone cost $65 million. Stacks of cannon-balls along the main entranceway give it the feel of a great stone fortress. Water cascades relentlessly into three-tiered swimming pools.

Across the highway from Ixtapa's main hotel strip is the ever-expanding La Puerta Shopping Center, a colorful Spanish-style complex of shops, boutiques, restaurants, and markets. AcaJoe's, Polo, Bazar La Guadalupana, Alberto's, Riba's—sportswear, jewelry, beachwear, handicrafts, silver, leather. While the shops in front ply their trade, those at the rear are still in various stages of construction. If you don't find what you want today, surely it will be there tomorrow.

Adding yet another dimension to the Ixtapa-Zihuatanejo development was the discovery several years ago of what is believed to be an ancient walled city thirty miles inland, deep in the dense jungle that lies between the ocean and the Sierra Madre. Several pre-Aztec societies inhabited the jungle lowland thousands of years ago. The discovery was made by a Mexicana airline pilot, who spotted the tops of ten gray stone temples from the air. News of the find spread quickly through the scientific community, and several international exploration groups were planning expeditions to the site. (The Ixtapa Club Med planned to offer scheduled tours.) But in the land of mañana, no one has yet hacked through the jungle. The discovery remains undiscovered.

Has glossy Ixtapa ruined Zihuatanejo's sleepy village appeal? Some changes are inevitable. Zihuatanejo tries feverishly to keep up with the blossoming giant next door. It even boasts a number of good hotels, most notably the Villa del Sol, a cluster of neo-Mediterranean bungalows on Playa la Ropa surrounding an open-air dining, bar, and pool area, all of which are run with exquisite taste by its German owner, Helmut W. Leins. But by and large, Zi-huatanejo remains characteristically unspoiled, impervious to all the development going on around it. Many of its restaurants still appear rustic enough to be life-threatening, and its handicraft shops reveal little indigenous talent.

Ixtapa's course is far more predictable. The top disco in town is Christine's, with its glittery interiors, lasers, mirrors, and flashing video images of Madonna. A group of about twelve people was kept cooling its heels outside behind a red velvet rope for nearly thirty minutes one night while I was there. When finally allowed to enter, the group found only about six other couples inside, amid the music, flashing lights, and empty tables.

As the newcomers ordered drinks, another group was already forming outside. Christine's will no doubt remain the hottest ticket in town for years to come.

The Yucatán Peninsula

*I*n Cozumel, where Mayan love gods once walked in their temples by the sea, a pair of young lovers sits on a deserted beach waiting for darkness to unite them. It's said that the island is still ruled over by the pagan deity Xchel, the goddess of fertility. At the brooding ancient temples of Uxmal and Chichén Itzá, big-beaked birds squawk noisily at the sudden change of light. Or perhaps a puma approaches.

The Maya reigned for more than 600 years, developing a highly sophisticated written language, constructing great pyramids and temples, and excelling in such complex abstract skills as astronomy, timekeeping, and mathematics. Known as the "Greeks of America," the Maya extended their influence into Guatemala, Honduras, and El Salvador. For reasons that are still obscure, the civilization collapsed about 900 A.D.

The Spanish of the Yucatán peninsula are Basque—proud, arrogant, strongly traditional people. Many of them still live in thick-walled villas with ornately grilled windows and enormous doors, large enough to suggest that perhaps giants live inside.

Mérida:
Hunting for a Turkey Made of Straw

*I*t seems I rarely travel anywhere these days without having the trip turn into a quest of some kind.

In Paris, I had to find a bottle of Bal de Versailles perfume for Alda. Had she told me what it cost, I wouldn't have looked so hard.

In Cairo, Felicity wanted me to find some henna, a dark reddish dye used for coloring hair (or, conceivably, other body parts to make them more alluring).

In Mexico, the quest is usually of my own making. In Puebla, I went all over town looking for place mats. I finally found them in Morelia while on another trip, hundreds of miles away. I found ceramic plates with Picasso-like faces in Dolores Hidalgo. A friend had bought some there and I had to have them.

Now I'm in Mérida looking for little turkeys made of straw. I have a small army of relatives coming for Thanksgiving dinner, and I thought they'd make ideal table favors that the guests could take home with them. I saw some here once, and they stayed in my mind. Now, while everyone else is off visiting pre-Columbian ruins and trudging through the museums, I'm looking for turkeys.

I went first to Milo's Casa de Monedas, just off the *zócalo,* or main square. I was told it's the place to go for antiques, religious carvings, coins, stamps, pottery, and dishware. But there were no turkeys. Besides, the place was pretty pricey. I looked at a small wooden crucifix; I could probably have bought a piece of the original for less.

Turkeys are a big deal in Mexico. Although U.S. citizens tend to think of the turkey as their own, especially at this time of year, Mexicans are equally possessive, and rightly so. The Aztecs of Mexico were enjoying turkey feasts long before the Spanish conquistadors ever got a whiff.

In most Latin American countries, the turkey is referred to by its Spanish name, *pavo,* but in Mexico it bears an Aztec name, *guajolote,* roughly derived from *hueyxoletl* or "important personage."

Just as the turkey is the bird of choice on Thanksgiving Day in the United States, turkey in *mole* sauce is frequently served on special occasions in Mexico, particularly at Christmastime. Turkey *mole* is the world's oldest known recipe. The Mayans ate it 9,000 years ago. Moctezuma served it to Cortés and his bunch.

I learned all this while talking to my old friend Alberto Salum, who owns Alberto's Continental Restaurant on Calle 57, not far from the *zócalo.* (Everything in Mérida is close to the *zócalo.*) The restaurant is housed in a 1727 hacienda and is filled with a trove of colonial paintings, santos (religious carvings), antique glazes, pottery pieces, and rare silver.

Proprietor Alberto Salum's grandparents came to Mexico from Syria. Menu specialties include multiple-course Arab meals as well as regional specialties such as chicken tamales and fish (snapper, sea bass, or other local catch) served Mayan style with rice and fried bananas.

Alberto told me that the native Mexican turkey is a hard-bitten, stringy-muscled strutter that walks hundreds of miles in its lifetime—perhaps the last mile right into the kitchen. Despite its scrawny appearance, it's bursting with flavor.

Nonetheless, turkey is almost always served with *mole* to give it more zip. Chile-based *mole* sauces come in dozens of varieties and flavors, like the chiles themselves, all of which change color as they ripen—red, yellow, brown, purple, green. Accordingly, the sauces come in various colors and tastes. *Moles* from Puebla are sweeter and milder than most, thanks to the influence of early Spanish nuns. In Tlaxcala, *moles* are hotter, thinner, and smoother than those found in Oaxaca, which tend to be heavy and exotic. (Connoisseurs will reject a *mole* that's too sweet before one that's too hot.)

At Alberto's, the turkey *mole* served on Monday is begun on Friday. It's pampered and prodded all weekend. Special ingredients are added, stirred, and allowed to fuse until finally, on Monday, perfection. The sauce is generally served over slices of roasted turkey, but again, recipes change from village to village, chef to chef.

Alberto is modest about his restaurant's tremendous success. Its more notable patrons have included President Jimmy Carter and actors Steve McQueen and Charlton Heston. But Alberto cautions that he doesn't want a lot of people showing up looking for celebrities. "It's not that kind of place," he says.

I eventually found my straw turkeys. The body is plain straw-colored, but the feathers and tail, also made of straw, are dyed red and green. There's a little bell inside, so each turkey forms a kind of rattle. I could just see my guests ringing the bell when they wanted more cranberry sauce or creamed onions. I couldn't wait to get them home.

They cost about a dollar each. I found them at a shop called Casa de las Artesanitas at Calle 63, No. 503. Not far from the *zócalo*.

Geographically cut off from the mainland, Mérida on the Yucatán peninsula has long resisted the intrusion of modern tourism.

Mérida's horse-drawn colonial carriages still clop across the Plaza de Independencia, where rays of sunlight filter through cathedral towers at sunset and spill into the sixteenth-century courtyard below.

Mérida is the capital of Yucatán, a peninsula that thrusts out from the Mexican mainland like the horn of a fighting bull, separating the Caribbean from the Gulf of Mexico. The city is twenty miles inland.

Rail and road links from Mérida to Mexico City were not completed until the 1950s. Before the highway was completed, anyone who wanted to go from Mérida to Mexico City had to sail to Veracruz and then proceed overland. Mérida residents found it easier to go to the United States or Cuba or Europe. Those influences can still be seen in the design and character of the city, regarded by some as the "Paris of the West."

Mérida was once the world's leading producer of henequen, a natural fiber related to sisal and used for making rope. Its landowners prospered in an atmosphere of tropical isolation. Now their sumptuous mansions along tree-shaded Paseo Montejo house mostly offices and restaurants.

A clean, safe city of 700,000, Mérida moves to a slow tempo, even for Mexico, better enabling visitors to savor its charms. But it is by no means backwards. When I dropped into a bookstore at the Dante Cultural Center on the Paseo de Montejo and inquired about a certain book, the young clerk ran to a computer to check. Upstairs was the ubiquitous coffee shop, where I had a bracing cappuccino.

Close by, the Anthropology and History Museum is located in another old mansion, the Palacio Canton, originally the governor's residence. Stone carvings, jade figures, and other Mayan relics and artifacts found in the area are displayed in the building's formal but homey atmosphere.

Some of the country's greatest archaeological sites are within a seventy-five-mile radius of Mérida. Dzibichaltun, twenty-five miles north of Mérida, is the oldest. It was built between 1200 and 100 B.C., and is only partially restored. Uxmal, purest of the Mayan ruins, is fifty miles south of Mérida. Only half a square mile in area, it offers a sweeping view of a compact, integrated city.

Chichén Itzá, seventy-five miles east of the Yucatán capital, is the largest and most popular of the ruins. It covers six square miles and contains twenty-five major structures, including an ancient ball court and El Castillo (The Castle), a temple pyramid that's seventy-five-feet tall and has 365 steps leading to its summit. All of the archaeological sites can be reached inexpensively by public bus, by rental car over good highways, or through hotel and local tour companies.

Mérida's showiest face is its plaza, where centuries-old laurel trees shade S-shaped Victorian benches known as *confidenciales*. The curves of their backrests separate the two people sitting on them. Romantic young couples could thus sit and converse at close quarters without upsetting their chaperons' sensibilities.

Lining the plaza are the governor's palace, the Cathedral of San

Idelfonso, the Casa de Montejo (built by the family that founded the city in 1542 and now a bank building), the Municipal Palace, and several shops and restaurants.

Just off the plaza is a small park that's illuminated in the evening by soft lights hanging from the trees. Here, outdoor restaurant tables are crowded, musicians play, and people come to see and be seen.

Cancún

*T*wenty-five years ago on Cancún, that slender stretch of island off Quintana Roo at the northernmost tip of the Yucatán peninsula, nothing existed beyond what Mother Nature put there.

And Mother Nature was generous indeed. Miles of pristine beaches were swept by the Caribbean on one side and gentle lagoons on the other. The colors of the sky and the water were the colors of Mayan jade, of gold and turquoise, colors that danced and shimmered in the changing light of day. In the late afternoon, when dark storm clouds sometimes gathered low in the sky, the colors intensified with such brilliance that ancient Indians considered this to be a place of wonderment and magic.

Today, the slender fourteen-mile-long elbow-shaped island of Cancún is the number-one tourist destination in all of Mexico, outdrawing even Acapulco with more than a million visitors a year. The hotel strip along Paseo Kukulcan—the busy central boulevard now known as the "Tourist Zone," where taxis and buses roar incessantly—looks like something out of Scheherazade's wildest dreams. Think of Las Vegas without neon. One mosquelike hotel with turrets and minarets stands next to another that resembles the keyboard of an IBM typewriter marching up a graded incline. Pyramids and towers with soaring atriums. Dozens and dozens of hotels—great dazzling sprawls of glass and steel and cement—all gleaming with excess and newness, all ribbon and wrapping. And everywhere you look are the skeleton-like frames of other hotels in various stages of completion. High up in one, a prematurely installed toilet and bath can be seen silhouetted against a naked blue sky.

The ever-changing room count, the barometer by which tourism officials measure a resort's success, staggers the mind. In 1988, Cancún had 11,891 rooms. By 1995, 18,500. By the century's end, an estimated 26,000 rooms in roughly 130 resort hotels will accommodate an anticipated 1.5 million visitors annually. Nowhere in the history of tourism has a resort of such record scale developed so quickly as here in the land of mañana. Not Miami Beach. Not Disney World. Not even Atlantic City with the advent of Donald Trump and gambling.

Quick to grasp the potential of Cancún's idyllic setting and sultry climate was Club Med. Designed along classic Mayan lines with stark white bungalows rising in tiers overlooking the shimmering lagoon, the Cancún Club Med was the first Club Med to open in Mexico (there are now five, with the village in Huatulco being the largest in the Western Hemisphere). Ever haughty and aloof, the property was built well away from all other Cancún development. But it's no longer isolated. Although not quite part of the hotel strip, the signs of encroachment are all around it.

Cancún's growth has been so rapid that the area already boasts an Old Cancún section downtown. The island, or hotel zone, is linked to the mainland by two inconspicuous causeways. It's downtown on the mainland that most of Cancún's 200,000 permanent residents live—the hotel waiters and bartenders, the taxi and bus drivers, the clerks, the accountants and secretaries, and their families.

The result of such growth, of course, is that much of the culture indigenous to this tip of Quintana Roo has disappeared. In the faces of the people on the street one sees little of the classic Mayan characteristics so prevalent elsewhere in Yucatán—the gentle oval face set with slightly protruding, coffee-bean–shaped eyes; full, sensuous lips; and a handsome beak of a nose. Nor does one see the typical Yucatán manner of dress—men in loose, white formless pants and shirts, their feet lashed into well-worn leather sandals; women in impeccably white sacklike dresses with gaily embroidered underskirts, called *huipiles,* peeking out from beneath the hems like petticoats. Even dolls and figurines of angels sold in the local shops are dressed that way. When I asked a saleswoman how the custom came about, she replied, "That's how the angels dress around here." Explanation enough, I suppose.

The modern Mayan Indians who comprised the main work force that constructed the buildings and hotels of Cancún are gone now, vanished much the way the ancient Mayans mysteriously disappeared in 900 A.D. There's no mystery about what happened to their modern-day descendants, however. They left Cancún because they couldn't compete for a living with the more skilled and educated workers and shopkeepers who were attracted to the big development boom at the tip of Quintana Roo.

According to Alfredo Cesar Dachary, director of the Research Center of Quintana Roo, developments such as Cancún are breeding a social crisis by creating islands of luxury in the midst of poverty. He calls the influx of tourists "the new conquistadors," citing the vacuum between the culture of the Mayans and the culture of Sheraton. Traditional Mayan cooking has been replaced by the likes of Bogart's, something akin to New York's 21 Club, San Francisco's Top of the Mark, and New Orleans's Chez Paul all rolled into one. Located in the Hotel Krystal on Punta Cancún, Bogart's recreates the atmosphere of the movie *Casablanca.* The Moorish-Moroccan design is emphasized with ceiling fans, high-backed rattan chairs, billowing silks, waiters in turbans, and giant photos of Bogart and Bacall that seem almost lifelike. Right there in the middle of it all sits a piano player in white tie and tails, stationed at a white piano, playing "As Times Goes By" over and over and over. Naturally, the experience comes with a price: $50 or more per dinner.

For American visitors accustomed to slick, clean resorts, these changes mean certain familiar creature comforts. Tourists can safely drink the water here and choose from a sometimes startling range of trendy restaurants that include Carlos'n Charlie's, the Bombay Bicycle Club, Casa Rolandi, La Mansión, Maxim's, the Hard Rock Cafe, Señor Frog's, and Mr. Papa's Potato House. The plaza in the town's center is filled with open-air bars and modern shops that include AcaJoe and many designer names. Jazz and country-western festivals featuring top names are now regular summer attractions.

Visitors can still find some Mexican touches in Cancún. At the open-air market one can haggle for silver jewelry, pottery, serapes, giant straw hats, and crafts. Weekly bullfights take place if enough tickets have been sold and the matador's plane makes it on time. Still, the place often has a hokey, touristy feel. Sometimes, Cancún seems about as authentically Mexican as your local taco restaurant.

So completely established has Cancún become as a resort that American visitors, like American travelers everywhere, can't wait to get somewhere else. Almost before their bags are unpacked, they're heading off to Isla Mujeres (Island of Women), a relatively undeveloped island six miles off the Cancún coast, to lounge on Playa Cocoteros, sip salty margaritas, or bum a ride on a fisherman's boat. Or they're taking the ferry or air shuttle to Cozumel, forty-four miles south of Cancún and twelve miles off the coast. Long a retreat for the fin-and-face-mask set—the diving is superb—Cozumel is more laid back, older, and considerably more Mexican than Cancún.

Other tourists jump into a car or bus and head down the highway to visit the ancient Mayan ruins of Tulum (located right on the sea, with a decent beach) or the lovely lagoon of Xel-Ha nearby. Or they go to the ruins of Chichén Itzá, about a two-and-a-half-hour drive from Cancún.

So great is the crush of traffic along Highway 180 to Chichén Itzá that the government has installed dozens of speed bumps along the way to keep drivers from whipping at life-threatening speeds through the tiny villages and settlements along the way. So many tour buses converge on Chichén Itzá that by midday it's almost impossible to find the entrance. People pour out of the buses wearing everything from safari jungle clothes to shorts and swimsuits. I saw two middle-aged European men in sagging bikinis accompanied by a lady with a parasol. The Yucatán sun can be brutal. Another woman with three kids in tow was crestfallen to learn that Mayaland was an old hotel close to the ruins and not an amusement park.

Inside the archeological site, people swarmed up and down El Castillo pyramid like ants on a hill, some frozen in terror at the top, others scampering goatlike up to the peak and down again. Troops of school children followed their instructors about, while official guides, voices weary with repetition, spoke of a phenomenon that takes place twice a year: During the spring and summer equinox, as the glowing red afternoon sun descends on the pyramid, its slanting rays form the shape of a giant serpent inching its way slowly down the stone steps until finally, with the advent of darkness, its massive head comes to rest at the base.

In the wake of Cancún's spectacular success, new resorts such as those at Akumal, Puerto Venturas, Buena Ventura, and Puerto Cancún have extended the development seventy-eight miles farther down the Yucatán coast.

Thankfully, the development hasn't ruined the place entirely, as I learned on the drive back from Chichén Itzá. I stopped at a roadside shack where a crudely lettered sign outside advertised "honey for sale." Unable to decide what kind of honey I wanted from among all the different sizes and shapes of bottles on display, I turned to the young man attending the shop for help. With a proud grin, he took my hand and poured a big puddle of honey into my open palm. "Try this one," he said. "It's good." And it was.

Like Pooh, I left the shack with several large jars of honey and continued along the highway toward Cancún. Still licking my hand, I suddenly felt confident that no matter how much development went on, no matter how big and grand and marvelous it became, somehow Cancún could never really be spoiled.

Chiapas

The town of San Cristóbal de las Casas is the main city in the Chiapas highlands and one of the prettiest cities in Mexico. With its red-tiled roofs, elegant mansions (some dating back to the time of the conquistadors), and narrow cobbled streets, it is every bit as charming as its native Indian market. Its 130,000 inhabitants seem to be mostly Mayan Indians who, though tiny, are dwarfed even more by the German and other European visitors who seem to be everywhere. Few Americans are evident. I asked someone who lived there why, when the people are so small, the sidewalks are so high? I'd never seen such high sidewalks. "In the rainy season," I was told, "it keeps the water from running into the houses and storefronts."

A silly thought came to mind as I wandered through the native handicraft stalls surrounding the ex-convent of Santo Domingo about four blocks north of the *zócalo* in San Cristóbal de las Casas. I was impressed with the endless array of crafts and merchandise devoted to the likeness of Subcomandante Marcos, who since 1994 has led a band of Indian rebels, demanding greater rights from the government for the people who originally inhabited the land. Wearing a black ski mask, a cartridge belt strapped across his chest, and a red bandana around his neck, the leader of the Zapatista rebels who emerged from the tangled jungles has become a cottage industry. Dolls, T-shirts, posters, little wooden trucks filled with Zapatista rebels, hair barrettes, earrings, belt buckles, ashtrays, books, photographs, and postcards all bear his likeness. Replicas of his familiar curved pipe and statues of his chestnut-colored horse,

Lucero, are for sale. During the 1910 Mexican Revolution, I wondered, did dolls and T-shirts champion the cause of Pancho Villa and Zapata? Times change.

I bought a doll, of course, outfitted with bullets and a ski mask.

"Do you collect dolls?" a lady writer from Austin asked, as though I had just been caught buying pantyhose. I assured her I did.

I was on a tour bus with a group of travel writers, all jockeying for a position in the pecking order of so-called professional journalists. Some produced a copy of their newest guidebook even before we'd left the airport terminal, where we were all meeting for the first time. Others were carrying scrapbooks of clippings, which we looked at with mild curiosity, reading a few lines of this and that, commenting politely. Sad to discover that there were no Paul Therouxs or Richard Fords in the group. There never are. I have learned to avoid anyone who gives a literal answer to a question asked in jest or who's afraid of political slogans on the wall.

A local official called me aside at dinner one night and said he could arrange an interview with Subcomandante Marcos for $150. It sounded reasonable. "A hundred fifty dollars?" I asked.

"No, no. *Eight* hundred fifty dollars."

I passed. You've got to wonder about somebody trying to avoid detection by wearing a ski mask in the steamy jungles.

The travel writers bus tour seems to go on forever. Villahermosa. It sounds like an American football team or a home for Norse gods. Tabasco. No relation to the hot sauce. El Greco rain clouds stretch across the horizon, keeping away the sun but not the promise that it's there. Rain puddles reflect the soft light. I hear somebody talking. "The only thing worse than the thought of waking up next to her in the morning is the thought of going to bed with her at night."

We speed along past jungle clearings with open *palapa*-roofed restaurants and music coming from tinny loudspeakers. I like to ride on buses with the windows open so I can feel the climate and smell the countryside. Odd that the most expensive buses in Mexico are the air-conditioned ones where the curtains all close so you can't see anything but the Sylvester Stallone movies playing on the overhead screens.

We speed on. Hovels along the road with bright pastel walls and geraniums in coffee cans. Cows munching on rich green grass, too busy to look up. We follow an open-bed truck filled with workers whose loose shirts flap in the wind, pushing the truck along like tiny sails.

At Palenque (the ruins not the cinder-block town that's grown up around it), a pretty girl in cut-off jeans and a white T-shirt poses against a tableau of timeless pre-Columbian splendor. A goddess in front of a disposable cardboard camera.

"Follow me," she calls to a friend.

"Until the end of time," I thought to myself. "To the ends of the earth."

Dusk comes. The darkening jungle smothers me like a coffin, and I suddenly feel that I have to leave, to go home, to stop traveling. But I can't.

3
Loose Pages from a
Writer's Portfolio

Frida and Diego: A Love Story

*W*hen the Frida Kahlo Museum finally reopened late in 1994—
after being closed for nearly two years for repairs and
remodeling—there was cause for celebration as well as for contro-
versy. The museum—Kahlo's family residence, which she shared
for twenty-five years with husband Diego Rivera (she was the third
of his four wives), was long a neglected gem among Mexico City
museums. The recent surge in popularity of Kahlo's work and a
fascination with her life suddenly brought huge crowds to the museum doors.

However, the general rundown condition of the building, height-
ened by the wear and tear of the growing number of visitors, proved
an embarrassment to Mexican officials. Because the roof leaked
badly, some fifty original Kahlo works on display had to be moved
for safekeeping to the Dolores Olmedo Foundation's new Diego
Rivera Museum in nearby Xochimilco.

Olmedo, one of Rivera's many loves and confidantes as well as his
most ardent collector, is the lifetime director of the Frida Kahlo Museum. However, when the renovation was extended for nearly two
years (the spectacular Museum of Anthropology in Chapultepec
Park took only nineteen months to construct from scratch), Kahlo
fans accused Dolores Olmedo of intentionally delaying the reopen-
ing out of lack of interest for the project or perhaps jealousy—
charges she ardently denied.

Olmedo pointed to walls and ceilings that had to be replaced and
floors that required fixing, as well as the painting of the museum's
exterior and interior and installation of new lights and a security

system. "It's an old house. It was falling down," she has said in an interview with the *Los Angeles Times.*

Located in the residential section of Coyoacán, on Londres and Allende streets, the museum immediately sweeps visitors into Kahlo's presence, which is everywhere. Painted a startling cobalt blue trimmed in red, the house has been preserved much as it was during the periods when Kahlo and Rivera lived there during the later years of their marriage. Its interior is filled with personal possessions and folk art—carved Indian masks, brightly colored *calaveras, retablos,* and pre-Columbian statuary. Beneath a death mask that hangs on the wall, a large, unmarked Mayan urn (behind glass now) contains Kahlo's ashes.

The exhibitions, museum officials note, have remained much the same—photographs, love letters, an address book opened to the New York address of a friend, financial ledgers, the four-poster bed in which Kahlo was born, a glass case filled with butterflies, and her collection of Japanese dolls. The brightly tiled kitchen is lined with Mexican ceramic ware; elsewhere are shelves of well-thumbed books on art, history, and politics. In the well-lighted studio a wheelchair is pulled up in front of an easel upon which rests an unfinished canvas of Joseph Stalin.

Other new additions include roped-off sections in the museum's interior, keeping the flow of visitors within specific areas. An electronic security system sounds an alarm if anyone wanders off or reaches beyond these restricted areas. A team of young female guides has replaced most of the surly guards who were previously posted throughout the museum. All students from the tourism school in Mexico City, the guides wear cobalt-blue uniforms matching the building's exterior, and neck scarves depicting a Frida Kahlo painting.

A ticket kiosk at the entrance has replaced the two welcoming twenty-foot-tall papier-mâché Judas figures, which were moved to the basement level. When Rivera gave the Kahlo residence to the Mexican government for use as a museum, it was with the stipulation that admission would always be free. But the Bank of Mexico (which operates the Diego Rivera Fiduciary and financed the renovation) decided to charge admission to help with the building's maintenance. (Dolores Olmedo, whose husband was a banker, has strong ties with the Bank of Mexico.) Attendance now averages 10,000 a month. A special Day of the Dead celebration in Frida Kahlo's honor annually attracts more than 1,500 visitors.

The spruced-up museum now has a gift shop (notably missing in the past) offering books, prints, posters, and postcards. On sale too are Frida Kahlo T-shirts and video cassettes of the award-winning Paul Leduc film, *Frida*. Also new are a library and a small coffee shop located at the basement level, off the back patio. Here visitors may peruse more than twenty Frida Kahlo biographies, ten on Diego Rivera, plus numerous other books, brochures, and magazine articles about Mexican art and the celebrated couple.

Kahlo's father, Guillermo, a German-Jewish emigrant who was a successful photographer, built the Coyoacán house for his family at the turn of the century. After marrying Frida, Rivera bought the land behind the house for a garden in which his young bride could work. A wall around the property was added years later, when the couple's fame had begun attracting crowds of the curious, anxious for a glimpse of them. Until then, only a cactus fence had separated the grounds from public view. Even the streets of Coyoacán were unpaved until the early 1950s.

When they lived in the Blue House, Casa Azul as it was called, Kahlo and Rivera formed the epicenter of contemporary art in Mexico, and around them, sparkling like fallout from a starburst, were some of the brightest and most creative personalities of the day. The Frida Kahlo Museum still attracts the fabled and the famed. Recent visitors have included Madonna, who purchased the film rights to a Frida Kahlo biography with plans to play the Frida role herself. Madonna owns several Frida Kahlo paintings including *My Birth*, which graphically depicts a stillborn infant unable to emerge from its mother's straining body. It hangs in her New York apartment. Lady Bird Johnson came to visit the museum with three of her nieces. Marcel Marceau came alone. The museum's manager, Laura Pérez Otero, has a photograph of herself and Richard Gere taken at the museum. Pure euphoria.

Although the Blue House has lost some of its former intimacy to museum-like efficiency, it is still an enchanted place, filled with sunshine, pain, and bright colors, the very essence of the artist herself.

More recently, in nearby San Angel, the Diego Rivera Studio Museum, the Mexican muralist's former home and workplace that he shared with Kahlo just after their marriage in 1929, took on new focus when the adjoining house was renovated and opened to the public for the first time. The two houses, connected by a second-floor walkway, illustrate the independence the couple maintained throughout their caring but unconventional union. Depending on their moods and whims at any given time, the highly complex, volatile couple frequently moved back and forth from the twin San Angel dwellings to the Kahlo family home in Coyoacán.

Considered the first example of avant-garde architecture in Mexico, the adjoining three-story houses were designed in Bauhaus style by artist Juan O'Gorman, a longtime friend of Rivera's. The second house, which was exclusively Kahlo's (Rivera liked lots of guests around; Kahlo preferred to work alone), had been closed for twenty-five years and was used primarily for storage. After extensive restoration, including an exterior coat of cobalt blue trimmed in red to match Frida's Casa Azul in Coyoacán, the house became part of what has been known since 1958 as the Diego Rivera Studio Museum. The combined facility is now called The Diego Rivera and Frida Kahlo Studio-House Museum.

Adjacent to the San Angel Inn restaurant in the trendy San Angel suburb of Mexico City, the main building is preserved much the way it was at the time of Rivera's death. The floor creaks, and the walls are covered with carved wooden masks, many with the price tags still dangling from them, indicative of a man too busy to remove them.

The cluttered studio is filled with tables and storage shelves covered with paint samples, plaster molds, and mounds of pre-Columbian statues and pottery that Rivera, an avid collector, bought by the kilo. Paintings, easels, and paint brushes are everywhere. In the bathroom is a stack of old frames. Off in a corner a large denim jacket hangs on a coat rack above a pair of paint-splattered shoes. Downstairs, exhibit space is devoted to changing exhibits by different artists.

When he designed and built the twin houses, O'Gorman went all out for his good friend Rivera. The buildings were ultramodern throughout, with tables, chairs, and furnishings made of polished steel. The cushions and upholstery were made of fine leather, colored in lime-green pastels. The window frames were constructed of structured steel. The work studios faced north to obtain the best lighting. The bedrooms faced south. There was an exhibit and sales gallery downstairs. Everything was new, modern, glittering, and in colors that only an artist could love—Indian red, indigo blue, orange, yellow, and parrot green.

Kahlo hated it. Her tastes leaned far more toward folk art and native Mexican designs. But she was a young bride and in love. The all-electric kitchen was too small—Who could cook with electricity anyway?—so Kahlo had a second, more traditional kitchen installed where she could enjoy making meals for her celebrated husband.

Says Blanca Garduno, director of the Diego Rivera Studio Museum, "We did considerable research of the period when Diego and Frida lived here and recreated the colors and furnishings. We're thrilled to have found nearly a dozen photos taken at the house, including one by Lola Alvarez Bravo and two by Nicholas Murray, one of Frida's early suitors who went on to become one of America's leading portrait photographers."

The German Bauhaus-inspired architectural style used by O'Gorman was known as "functionalism." Its objective was to economize space, a plan that in hindsight seems almost redundant in Mexico, a country where families are large and dwellings are small. Rivera's small bedroom doubled as a changing room for models and a place to store pigeon food. There was also room for servants and guests—María Hernandez, the maid, lived on the lower level and took care of the studio, and Sixto, the driver who drove Diego's old Ford pickup and served as a busboy and helper, slept on a straw mat near the front door.

Ruth and Guadalupe, Rivera's children from his second wife,

Lupe Marin, were frequent visitors, as was Marin herself, who became one of Kahlo's closest friends.

In the center of it all, between the tables, chairs, sofas, and paint was that whirlwind of creativity known as Diego Rivera.

Wrote Kahlo, "Always working, Diego does not live a life that could be called normal. His capacity for energy shatters clocks and calendars. Physically, he lacks time for the struggle, without rest, planning and constantly producing work."

Rivera earned his reputation through mural painting but paid his bills with easel and portrait commissions. He commissioned the twin houses with money earned from the painting *La elaboración de un mural* done in the United States. Some of his most famous works were completed at the San Angel studio, including *Nude with Gannets, The Painter's Studio, Portrait of Dolores Olmedo, Woman in White,* and *The Watermelons.* It was also here that he painted family portraits reflecting love and tenderness. Some of Kahlo's more notable works were done here as well, including *The Two Fridas, Self-Portrait with Monkey, The Fruit of the Land,* and *Little Dead Dimas.*

Their home became something of a mecca for intellectuals of the day—writers Pablo Neruda, André Breton, John Dos Passos, and Waldo Frank; artist Henry Moore; photographers Edward Weston and Manuel Alvarez Bravo; celebrated actresses Dolores del Rio, María Felix, and Paulette Goddard.

Among the many famous houseguests were film star Edward G. Robinson and his wife, Gladys. While Kahlo entertained Mrs. Robinson on the roof terrace of her house, Rivera, always his wife's biggest fan, showed the actor some of her paintings. Robinson bought four of them for $200 each. At the time it was Kahlo's most substantial sale.

It is difficult to imagine Rivera, who weighed more than 300 pounds when he and Kahlo were married, moving through the functionalist studio, which had only a small bedroom and bathroom and minuscule stairs. The steep, winding stairs eventually proved too much for the physically impaired Kahlo to manage (childhood polio and a serious streetcar accident left her considerably handicapped), and the couple finally moved back to the Blue House, her family home in Coyoacán. Rivera kept the studio in San Angel as his workplace and, virtually bedridden during the last few months of his life, it was there that he died.

Rivera's daughters, Ruth and Guadalupe, continued to live in the house after Rivera's death, remodeling and making additions as they saw fit. The Mexican Government bought the property from them in 1986.

It is not surprising that the San Angel home would be unveiled as yet another Kahlo shrine. Interest in her life and work of late, known within art circles as "Fridamania," has been nothing short of phenomenal. Recently, Kahlo's *Self-Portrait with Monkey and Parrot* sold for $3.2 million, the highest price ever paid at auction for a Latin American painting. It originally sold in 1947 for $400.

It was a longtime interest in the work of Diego Rivera that brought me to the Frida Kahlo Museum for the first time. I had anticipated little more than a footnote of insight into Rivera's life. Yet I was overwhelmed by what I saw.

The museum was still virtually unknown in the late 1980s. In mounting frustration, the taxi driver drove up one street and down another before finally pulling up in front of a nondescript gray building that he insisted was the address I wanted. I entered what appeared to be a deserted elementary school cafeteria.

As I turned to leave, I was startled by a dark-haired woman coming toward me from the far side of the dimly lit room. She was on crutches. My heart almost stopped—she looked like Frida Kahlo herself. With a deep, throaty laugh, the woman apologized for having frightened me and directed me to my destination, a one-story stucco structure a few blocks away.

Crippled by polio as a child, Frida Kahlo was further handicapped in adolescence by a streetcar accident that shattered her pelvis and spine. As a result, the artist spent much of her life bedridden, on crutches, or in a wheelchair.

The more than fifty paintings and drawings on display at the time—most are now at the Dolores Olmedo Museum—comprised the largest single collection of her work. (Kahlo left behind fewer than 200 paintings in all.) Despite critical acclaim during her lifetime—and major shows in Mexico City, Paris, and New York—Kahlo's work fell into obscurity after her death. But it has resurfaced during the past few years. Exploded would be more accurate. Like the desert century plant, whose roots and stalk are already dead or dying when it finally bursts into glorious bloom, Frida Kahlo is in full flower.

Her work is everywhere today. Vanguard of an unprecedented worldwide boom in Latin American art, her tormented self-portraits (Frida wearing a crown of thorns to show her suffering, Frida with her exposed heart worn like a religious medal) today grace magazine covers as well as museum walls, films, books, videos, and television documentaries.

In Mexico City, I saw one sidewalk entrepreneur selling necklaces made from flattened bottle caps—each disk embedded with a photo of Frida.

The Frida Kahlo resurgence began in 1977, when the Mexican government mounted a retrospective exhibit of her work at the prestigious Palacio de las Bellas Artes—the Palace of Fine Arts—in Mexico City. In 1978 the exhibition traveled to museums in six U.S. cities. Other Kahlo paintings have since drawn crowds in museums and galleries around the world.

Exposure for Kahlo and her art increased with the publication in 1983 of *Frida,* a well-regarded biography by Hayden Herrera (Harper and Row). *Time* magazine called it "a mesmerizing story of radical art, romantic politics, bizarre loves, and physical suffering." The groundswell continued in 1985 with the opening of the biographical play *The Two Fridas* at the Teatro Julio Prieto in Mexico City. This was followed by director Paul Leduc's stunning film *Frida,* which opened to enthusiastic audiences in the United States. It stars the uncanny Kahlo look-alike, Ofelia Medina, who won the 1985 Latin American Film Festival's best-actress award in Havana for her portrayal.

Virtually devoid of dialogue, *Frida* unfolds in a series of eloquent, deathbed flashbacks. The haunting tableaux and images that drift back and forth in time include a spirited pillow fight between Frida and her father; her illness with childhood polio; the devastating streetcar accident; her involvement in political rallies; tender scenes with Diego, including one in which he sings to her from his mural scaffolding; a Day of the Dead celebration; and the invalid's painful, pensive moments alone.

The scene of the crippling accident is particularly graphic. In 1925, eighteen-year-old Magdalena Carmen Frida Kahlo y Calderón, pursuing a medical career at the time, was returning home from the exclusive National Preparatory School in Mexico City when her bus was struck by an electric streetcar. Kahlo's abdomen was pierced by one of the train's iron handrails. Her spine and pelvis were fractured, and her left arm and right leg and foot were broken. Kahlo would never fully recover from the massive injuries, and many of her artworks reflect her ensuing physical pain.

"Frida's life from 1925 on was a grueling battle against slow decay," writes biographer Herrera. "She had a continuous feeling of fatigue, and almost constant pain in her spine and right leg. There were periods when she felt more or less well and her limp was almost unnoticeable, but gradually her frame disintegrated.

"A lifelong friend," Herrera continues, "says that Frida had at least thirty-two surgical operations, most of them on her spine and right foot, before she succumbed twenty-nine years after the accident. 'She lived dying,' said writer Andres Henestrosa, another close friend for many years."

But it was the accident that launched Kahlo's career as an artist. As the artist herself once wrote, "I never thought of painting until 1926, when I was in bed on account of [the] accident. I was bored as hell in bed with a plaster cast (I had a fracture in the spine and several in other places), so I decided to do something. I stoled [sic] from my father some oil paints, and my mother ordered for me a special easel . . . and I started to paint." Using mirrors, she became her own model—beginning to produce the self-portraits for which she is best known.

Kahlo quickly developed her own distinct style, relying heavily on her Mexican background, rooted in both Indian and Roman

Catholic imagery. She was an artist's artist. French surrealist poet André Breton once compared her work to a "bomb with a ribbon tied around it." Kandinsky saw her work for the first time and broke into tears. Picasso, whom she met in Paris in 1939, presented her with handsome earrings—little hands—of his own design. (She wears them in two of her famous self-portraits.) Diego Rivera declared her the greatest artist of her time, describing her style as "agonized poetry."

At first glance, the couple couldn't have seemed more mismatched. Tiny, delicate Frida was twenty-two when she married the forty-three-year-old Rivera in 1929. Throughout their years together she hid her crippled leg beneath long peasant skirts and disguised the anguish of numerous operations and miscarriages with a rainbow of bright colors—ribbons and braids in her hair; Indian blouses; swirls of beads; large, ornate earrings; flamboyant corsages. The exotic-looking Kahlo was not only an artist but a work of art herself. (She is said to have been photographed even more often than Marilyn Monroe.)

Rivera, on the other hand, was a towering giant with a huge stomach and bulging eyes (self-admittedly the face of a frog). He frequently carried a gun, had to be reminded to bathe, and often arrived at important social receptions directly from his mural scaffolding, wearing paint-splattered overalls. In Kahlo's famous wedding portrait, Rivera looks immense next to his bride—and he was. Six feet tall, he weighed 300 pounds. Frida was five foot three inches and weighed ninety-eight pounds. Rivera, with his palette and brushes, is portrayed as the artist he was, while Frida stands at his side as his adoring wife.

Yet husband and wife fought, squabbled in public, and relentlessly cheated on each other. Rivera had an affair with Frida's younger sister, Christina. Frida once bedded Leon Trotsky, a guest at their Coyoacán home. (The revolutionary must have been an understandably nervous lover, with one eye out for the pistol-packing Rivera and the other for would-be assassins.) Frida also had a number of affairs with women.

Kahlo and Rivera divorced in 1939, only to remarry the following year on the groom's fifty-fourth birthday. Although the second union was as traumatic and episodic as the first, it was tinged with Diego's care and tenderness in the face of Frida's declining health. In 1953, gangrene forced the amputation of Kahlo's right leg. The artist died a year later of a pulmonary embolism, six days before her forty-seventh birthday.

Rivera was devastated. At the funeral he ate a handful of her ashes and vowed that when the time came, he would also be cremated and that their ashes would be mixed together so they would be as one forever. But his wish never came to pass. When Rivera died three years later, he was awarded Mexico's highest honor by being buried at Rotonda de los Hombres Ilustres in Mexico City.

Certainly, few famous artists have been as autobiographical in their work as Kahlo, whose paintings unfold like the pages of a bittersweet diary. Providing searing glimpses into the artist's life, they are brilliantly colored, brutally direct, and deceptively childlike. The self-portraits range from early images capturing the pleasures, fantasies, and humor of a blossoming young woman who enjoyed many of life's advantages, to those expressing despair caused by chronic physical pain and numerous disappointments in love and life. (Kahlo wanted to have a child by Rivera, but she never succeeded in carrying one to term.)

One dominating theme in Kahlo's work is her obsession with her own body. Indeed, Kahlo's tormented self-portraits frequently probe deep beneath her skin, depicting blood, arteries, and exposed organs in gruesome detail. The scenes are clearly surrealist, marked by symbolic complexity.

The tender but philandering Rivera was also a focus of much of Kahlo's work. He appears time and time again, from the wedding portrait—painted in the nineteenth-century Mexican folk-art style—to the childlike figure of Diego held by his wife in *The Love Embrace of the Universe*. It was Rivera's affair with Frida's sister that inspired the particularly horrifying painting, *A Few Small Nips,* in which the figure of a man wielding a knife stands over a woman's stabbed and mutilated body. Blood is painted even on the frame. Kahlo obviously saw Rivera's betrayal as butchery.

Confined so often to her home by illness, Frida filled the house and garden with a noisy menagerie of spider monkeys, Mexican hairless dogs, parrots, an osprey, deer, cats, and an armadillo. In various symbolic guises, the creatures come to inhabit her paintings as well. In one, death appears over the artist's shoulder in the form of a black cat. In another, *The Little Deer,* Kahlo depicts herself as a hunted, wounded animal pierced with arrows.

Yet the proclivity toward blood and mutilation in Kahlo's work probably can be attributed less to pain or self-absorption than to the Mexican fascination in general with death, dying, and the macabre.

The Two Fridas is Kahlo's largest and perhaps best-known work. Painted during the time of her divorce from Rivera, it contains two full-length self-portraits on a single canvas—the Frida he loved and the one he spurned. Against a turbulent sky reminiscent of El Greco's *View of Toledo,* the two Fridas sit side by side on a bench, holding hands as though to comfort one another. The rejected Frida wears a white Victorian dress, spotted with blood. The other Frida is darker, more Indian-looking, and wears native, peasant-style clothing. This duality in Frida's personality is frequently revealed in her work. The painting hangs in the Museum of Modern Art in Mexico City, and a full-sized replica in black and white can be seen at the Frida Kahlo Museum in Coyoacán. Two ceramic clocks in the dining room represent Frida's despair at the time. The clocks mark the hour and the day of the couple's divorce ("Time Stopped Here," reads the inscription) and of their remarriage the following year.

Other Kahlo works inspired by traditional Mexican art are done in the style of *retablos,* miracle paintings on tin that usually contain a written legend on the bottom requesting spiritual intervention in a time of crisis or giving thanks when such help is granted. Perhaps most notable of these is her *Suicide of Dorothy Hale.* On October 21, 1938, Hale, a fading socialite and former Ziegfeld Follies showgirl, gave a dinner party in her apartment high above Central Park South in New York City. After her guests had left, she committed suicide by jumping out the window. Clare Booth Luce, editor of *Vanity Fair* at the time, commissioned Kahlo, a mutual friend, to paint a memorial portrait for Hale's mother. Frida painted the scene of the suicide in *retablo* style, with images of Hale jumping out of the window, falling through the air, and finally lying dead on the ground, blood spilling from her mouth. When Luce saw the painting, she was horrified and demanded that it be destroyed. She later acceded to having her name removed from the *retablo's* caption and, smeared name and all, the painting survives today.

Arguably, the work of almost any modern painter might be viewed as a deposition for psychotherapy, but none more so than Frida Kahlo's. Salomon Grimberg, M.D., the noted psychiatrist and Mexican art scholar who curated a 1989 Kahlo exhibition at the Meadows Museum in Dallas, claims that Kahlo's art is "charged with a negative energy that can destroy. People who are very involved with the work of Frida Kahlo are contaminated by this energy," says Grimberg, who became fascinated by Kahlo's art twenty years ago. "That's why I'm through with her. I could live with her paintings forever, but they suck you dry.

"She has a self-absorbing, morbid preoccupation," Grimberg continues. "She paints herself with childlike vulnerability. She's always looking out at you with these hungry eyes. She's always saying, 'Feed me. I'm hurting.'"

Thus, from an analyst's couch may come the summation of the pain and passion of Frida Kahlo. She was in love with life and wanted desperately to be loved in return.

Portrait of Lupe Marin

*E*xamining Diego Rivera's work, one is always impressed with the artist's eye for beautiful women, both as subjects for his paintings and for his amorous pursuits—Dolores del Rio, Paulette Goddard, María Felix, and Frida of course. But none compared to Lupe Marin, Rivera's second wife.

In the words of Bertram Wolfe, Rivera's biographer: "Long of limb and tall of body, as graceful and as supple as a sapling; hair black, wild unkempt, curly; dark olive skin, light sea-green eyes, high forehead and nose of a Phidian statue; full lips ever parted by eager breath and by lively, disorderly and scandalous chatter; a body so slender as to suggest a youth rather than a woman—such was Lupe when Diego met her."

She also caught the eye (and the lens) of photographer Edward Weston, who described her as "tall, proud of bearing, almost haughty; her walk was like a panther's, her complexion almost green, with eyes to match—gray-green, dark circled, eyes and skin such as I have never seen."

Guadalupe Marin was from Guadalajara, a city known for its beautiful women. Diego first met her when he hired her to model as the nude figure in his *Creation* mural at the National Preparatory School, one of his first major commissions. (Frida Kahlo was a student of sixteen at the school at the time.)

Rivera described his first meeting with Lupe: "A strange creature of a marvelous countenance, almost six feet tall, appeared. She had black hair, but her hair seemed more like that belonging to a chestnut mare than to a woman. Her green eyes were so transparent that she seemed blind."

In a pattern that was to repeat itself often throughout Rivera's career, the model soon became his mistress.

Lupe appeared as the earth figure in Rivera's chapel mural at the Universidad Autónoma de Chapingo. He also painted numerous portraits of her during and after their marriage.

They were married in the Church of San Miguel in Guadalajara in 1922. He was thirty-five. Lupe was twenty, and she was an independent and strong-willed woman from the start. "Rivera may be a great painter," clucked the neighbor women, "but his wife carries her own basket in the market, like an Indian."

She was also tempestuous. Rivera had little regard for his marriage vows, and the high-strung, high-spirited Lupe wasn't about to let her philandering husband stray in peace. She caused scenes in public, tore up his drawings, and once threatened to shoot off his right arm with his own gun so he could never paint again. One night when he was late for dinner and she suspected he was out carousing, Lupe smashed two of his favorite pieces from his pre-Columbian pottery collection and served them to him at dinner that night in his soup.

Not surprisingly, the marriage, though it produced two daughters, Ruth and Guadalupe, was short-lived. It simply dissolved after Rivera went to Paris to study with some of the French masters. Because they had only been married in the church, the marriage wasn't legally binding at any rate. Lupe found someone else, and Rivera, who had since returned to Mexico, discovered Frida Kahlo, or rather she discovered him.

When Diego and Frida decided to marry, Lupe (who remained on good terms with Diego) helped with the wedding reception. At one point during the festivities, she became annoyed at all the attention being paid to Frida. She went to the couch where Frida was sitting, raised the skirt of the startled young bride, and said, "And for these crooked legs, he left me." Then she stormed out of the house.

But in the months that followed, Lupe and Frida became good friends. Lupe, who was an excellent cook, taught Frida how to prepare the meals that Diego favored. Ruth and Guadalupe were frequent visitors to the couple's San Angel home, and Frida loved them as her own.

When Frida died in 1954, the first person the devastated Diego Rivera called with the sad news was Lupe Marin.

Mexican Food: You Are What You Eat

When you order breakfast in Mexico, skip the pancakes and order *huevos rancheros* instead—two fried eggs on a tortilla, bathed in hot sauce. Refried beans come with it and a slice of tomato garnished with fiery bits of jalapeño peppers. It's a meal calculated for get up and go.

Not all Mexican food is hot, but all Mexican food is good. And it's good for you. Experts say that the basic staple diet of the Mexican peasant is among the healthiest in the world.

Beans provide carbohydrates and protein. Corn, from which tortillas are made, offers protein and calcium. Chiles, used in everything Mexican, are one of the most versatile seasonings known and contain an entire warehouse of vitamins and minerals. They're particularly loaded with vitamin C.

This food so impressed Cortés when he arrived in Mexico in 1517 that he sent large quantities back to Spain. "Sight of sights," he thought when he saw Indians eating beans scooped up on a flat tortilla. "Not only do they eat the food," he said, "but they eat the plates as well."

Archaeological evidence indicates that beans, corn, and chiles have been the mainstay of the Mexican diet for at least 7,000 years. In the Mayan legend of creation, the same corn dough used in making tortillas was used to make the first edition of Man. The gentle, rhythmic pat-pat-pat of tortillas being made is one of the most characteristic sounds of Mexico, as it has been for centuries. Aztec children were asked a riddle: What is it that goes along the foothills of the mountains patting out tortillas? A butterfly.

Despite the recent incursion of packaged and processed foods, the bean, corn, and chile triad continues to be a Mexican staple. A corn tortilla, hot off the stove, filled with beans and laced with a sauce of ground chiles, herbs, and red tomatoes, is a treat as tasty as it is timeless.

The oldest known recipe for cooked food existing in the world today is turkey and *mole* sauce, *mole de guajolote.* The Mayans ate it 9,000 years ago. Moctezuma served it to Hernán Cortés. The chief components of the original recipe were chiles, green and red tomatoes, corn dough or tortillas, squash seeds, peanuts, and cacao. It's said that the nuns of the Santa Rosa convent in Puebla embellished the original recipe to please a visiting viceroy, adding bread to thicken the sauce and almonds for taste. The tiled, high-ceiling kitchen where they worked is a popular museum today, filled with gleaming copper pots, cooking utensils, and colorful ceramic dish-ware.

Much of the appeal of Mexican food is in its texture. When you bite into a crispy taco packed with strips of meat or chicken, shredded lettuce, chopped onion, sliced radishes, bits of olive, and grated *queso fresco*, all doused with spicy sauce, your taste buds dance with an explosion of flavor. *Pan,* Mexican bread, has the heft and feel of bread that has never known a chemical preservative. It's made in dry, flour-dusted places where the smell is comforting and warm.

Such devotion to taste is typical of Mexican cooking. *Chiles rellenos,* for instance, is Mexico's version of stuffed peppers. But how they're stuffed! First the broad *poblano* chile pepper is toasted over an open fire until its paper-thin outer skin blisters and can be easily removed. Its seeds and veins are discarded. Then the pepper is filled with an extraordinary mixture of meat, garlic, vinegar, clove, black pepper, a dash of vanilla, saffron, cumin, nutmeg, blanched almonds, raisins, candied citrons, and a slice of fat, all of which has been boiled together until almost dry. Thus impregnated, the pepper is then dipped in egg batter and fried until light and golden. There are variations, the most popular being peppers stuffed with farmer's cheese.

Even frijoles, cooked and crushed to the consistency of mashed potatoes, refried in a few ounces of bacon fat, and topped with a dash of melted cheddar cheese, reach a perfection of taste rarely achieved of the lowly bean anywhere else in the world. Occasionally, a small river of pumpkin seed oil is poured on top in place of the cheese. For centuries, pumpkins have been grown in Mexico only for the flavor of their rich, nutty seeds. The rest is thrown away.

The chiles used so frequently in Mexican cooking are as varied as the food itself. More than ninety varieties exist, and they tend to cross-pollinate, leading to variations of variations. Soil can also alter taste, just as the taste of grapes from one vineyard will change when the vines are transplanted to another vineyard.

Contrary to popular belief, hot chile peppers are not at all harmful to normal digestive systems. Quite the opposite. Capsaicin, the alkaloid element in chiles that causes the sensation of burning, is often used by pharmaceutical firms as a local counter-irritant and as a gastric stimulant.

Generally, the smaller chiles such as the serrano and the thumb-sized jalapeño are the hottest. But fear not. The fire is excellent for the digestion. It causes the flow of saliva to protect the tongue tissues and sets off the flow of gastric juices, stimulating the appetite.

The place to go to begin your search for good Mexican food is Mexico City—ah, Mexico City—in the old district near the Zócalo. (Residents of Mexico City suggest that the old district is not the safest place to be at night and that its restaurants might best be visited for lunch.)

The Hostería de Santo Domingo at Belisario Domínguez 72 is believed to be the oldest restaurant in the city. It opened in 1860. The restaurant's late owner, Gustavo Orozco, began there as a waiter more than thirty-five years ago. It was he who took me over to another table one night to meet fellow diner Rufino Tamayo, the famous Mexican painter. Awed and somewhat at a loss for words, I asked the white-haired artist to autograph my menu, and he cheerfully obliged, scrawling his impressive signature right across the *pollo en mole poblano,* chicken in *mole* sauce. Tamayo died in the summer of 1991 at the age of ninety-one. I'll never part with the menu.

Gustavo's son, Sergio, now runs the restaurant, which is said to have a resident ghost lurking about upstairs, but then there are lots of ghosts in Mexico.

The Café de Tacuba is also a throwback to another era with its elaborate chapel-like entranceway, ornately tiled walls, and brass chandeliers. It was founded in 1912 by Dionisio Molinedo of Tabasco. Huge brooding colonial portraits stare down at diners as waitresses in crisp white uniforms and ruffled caps hurry about.

It was in Café de Tacuba where Diego Rivera, wife Frida Kahlo, and friends were dining one night when at a nearby table Deputy Altamirano, "the next governor of Veracruz," was gunned down by assassins. According to his biographer Bertram Wolfe, Rivera watched the scene with an expression of "excited exaltation" on his face. He went directly to his studio that night and emerged the next morning with a finished painting of the assassination scene, exact in every detail.

No shootings have occurred there lately, however. Café de Tacuba is always busy and noisy, with the constant clatter of silverware, the snap of bottles opening, and the chatter of patrons all resounding against the tile walls. Tasty soups, chicken dishes, and a score of daily specials are offered.

Sanborn's, not far away on Madero in the landmark House of Tiles building, is another timeless retreat. Its original open courtyard, where horse-drawn carriages used to arrive, is closed in now. Refracted light from the glass ceiling sets the mood each day. As spacious as a train terminal, with balconies above for shopping, browsing, or people-watching, the restaurant was the first in the now-nationwide Sanborn's chain. For years it was the home-away-from-home for such noted foreign visitors as authors D. H. Lawrence and B. Traven, Russian film director Sergei Eisenstein, and photographer Edward Weston who, writing in his journal in August 1923, expressed displeasure with changes at Sanborn's. "What was once a marvelous palace of blue tiles has been redecorated, turned into a typical American restaurant."

A fire in 1998 closed the restaurant for several months for repairs. The renovation includes a new bistro and an additional upstairs dining room. A famed Orozco mural over the rear stairwell was undamaged.

Just up the street on Tacuba is Los Girasoles. The name means "sunflowers," and you know how artists go crazy for sunflowers. A regular here is José Luis Cuevas—one of his large paintings is at the far end of the bar; he always eats upstairs, however, for privacy. The restaurant is convenient to the José Luis Cuevas Museum, in the former Convent of Saint Ines behind the National Palace. Los Girasoles is also right next door to the National Art Museum, and that too brings in an arty crowd. The restaurant—its bright yellow colonial-style building bedecked with flags and flower boxes, with umbrella-shaded tables spilling out onto the sidewalk—is dazzling. But some might find it too snobby for words.

The San Angel Inn restaurant in San Angel, with its beamed ceilings, cozy fireplaces, and lush gardens, is another popular favorite. Order a margarita at the San Angel Inn and it arrives in an individual silver decanter, gleaming with icy beads of condensation.

Originally a Carmelite monastery and the former home of the first Spanish ambassador to Mexico, the San Angel Inn touches all phases of Mexican history. Zapata and Pancho Villa formalized their famous pact, dividing jurisdiction between the north and south of Mexico, within its walls while their horses were watered in the patio fountain. While a guest at the San Angel Inn, the actress Paulette Goddard is said to have had a blazing affair with Diego Rivera, whose studio across the street is now a museum.

Prendes, near the Latin American Tower, one of Mexico's finest seafood restaurants, opened in 1892. Many of its most famous patrons have been immortalized in a huge Castellano wall mural. Over a bowl of steaming *caldo largo de alvarado* (seafood soup with chiles and tomatoes), you can pick out matadors Carlos Arruza and Manolete, actor Gary Cooper, Pancho Villa, Santa Anna, Caruso, and Walt Disney for an unlikely assortment of dinner companions.

I ate alone there one night and was given a seat far in the back, a section where the waiters congregate after the evening rush to undo their bow ties, smoke, spoon a bowl of soup, or count their tips. In the pale gray evening light that's so particular to Mexico City both indoors and out, they seemed to be more of a painted tableau than the mural on the wall.

The restaurant scenes in Paul Leduc's award-winning movie, *Frida,* were filmed at Prendes. Leon Trotsky had his last meal there.

Also highly popular, and justly so, is Fonda el Refugio in the trendy Zona Rosa, where Mexican specialties are served in warm, pleasant surroundings. *Carne asada,* thin fillets of broiled beef in chile sauce, and *mole verde de pepita,* poached chicken with a green sauce made of pureed pumpkin seeds and chiles, get especially high marks.

Fonda el Refugio is popular with artists as well as Mexican soap opera stars. You can always spot the latter because their eyelashes are long enough to blow out all the candles on the tables with a simple whisk.

Gleaming copper pots, ceramic pottery, antique carvings, tiles, photos of famous regulars with their gushing inscriptions, and an entrance wall covered with *retablos* are all part of the appeal of Fonda el Refugio.

Tequila

*T*ake a country whose daily basic diet of tortillas, frijoles, enchiladas, and jalapeño peppers could power a Boeing 747, and it
only stands to reason that it would produce a fiery liquor that tastes
as if it were distilled by the gods.

Almost all tequila produced in Mexico comes from the town of
Tequila in the state of Jalisco. There in the mile-high subtropical
climate grows the maguey *azul,* the blue maguey. Tequila is distilled from the juice of this giant, spiny-leafed member of the ama-
ryllis family. The plants, more than 100 million of them, cover the
parched foothills of the Sierra Madre west of Guadalajara in metic-
ulous rows, roughly 1,200 to an acre. Each plant takes eight to ten
years to reach maturity, at which time its spiny leaves are hacked
off and its pineapple-like heart *(piña),* weighing 80 to 120 pounds,
is removed and trucked off to a distillery.

Of the more than fifty tequila factories in the state of Jalisco,
most are minor operations. About ten companies, largely those in
the town of Tequila, account for three-fourths of the total production. Tequila Sauza, a firm founded in 1873, and José Cuervo are
the two giants.

Tequila is part of the soul of Mexico. Behind the swinging doors
of the cantinas in every town and crossroad of Mexico, it is potent
tequila that reduces the cares and disappointments of the day to a
benevolent shrug. It has done so, albeit in a more primitive form,
since the Aztecs first fermented the sap of the spiny maguey to
make a milky, slightly foamy drink called "pulque." Ancient
murals at the site of the Great Pyramid of Cholula, seventy miles

east of Mexico City, show pulque drinkers kicking up their sandals and having a marvelous time as far back as 200 A.D. Clay pulque cups known as *cazuelas* are common among pre-Columbian terra cotta finds.

Pulque was used primarily during religious celebrations and festivals and provided numerous medical remedies, not the least of which was its strong tranquilizing effect. In pre-conquest culture, when drunkenness was a crime punishable by death, old people and nursing mothers were permitted pulque's continued use because of its high nutritive qualities. The first pharmaceutical writings of the New World (the Cruz-Badiano codex) described sixteen potions with pulque as an ingredient. White, like milk, the pulque sap was a gift from the gods, according to legend; it was sucked by mouth from the plants and allowed to ferment. Peasant Indians of Mexico still use pulque as a major home remedy. Medical herbs are often mixed with pulque to increase their benefits. In rural Mexico, *pulquerías* are the main watering holes, and they're purely a male domain, with open urinals often running the length of one wall.

Throughout Mexico it's not surprising to find tequila being sold in pharmacies and hardware stores as well as in the local grocery stores and liquor shops. It is said to contain certain properties that can cure or arrest the effects of syphilis, purify the blood, and act as an aphrodisiac. It is also used as an astringent for cuts and bruises, an aftershave lotion, an insect repellent, a lighter fluid for charcoal fires, and when used in moderation, a cholesterol fighter. It's considered a digestive aid, a diuretic, and a laxative all in one and is appropriately served before, during, or after meals. It's so rich in yeast and vitamins that nursing mothers frequently apply several drops to the breast to perk up the baby. All of which may explain the uncommon sense of warmth and well-being one frequently encounters upon entering a Mexican cantina.

It was the hard-drinking Spanish conquistadors—their supply of wines and brandy quickly exhausted—who managed to distill the maguey sap into 110-proof mescal, a potent forerunner of tequila.

Some brands of mescal are still sold today with a worm or caterpillar floating at the bottom of the bottle, a custom initiated by Aztec priests to instill in the drink a life spirit of its own. The worm is highly prized as an aphrodisiac by today's mescal drinker, the great majority of whom are Mexican peasants. (Mescal is considerably cheaper than tequila.) Very little mescal is sold in the United States.

Tracking tequila to its source, to the town of Tequila itself, will disappoint most visitors. The highway from Guadalajara narrows to two lanes most of the way and appears to be used almost exclusively by diesel trucks, buses, and pickup trucks. Chicken farms and a scattering of houses and small factories give way to the endless maguey fields and finally to the town itself. Its dusty, unpaved streets are lined with mud-brick houses and surrounded by rolling hills that seem to stretch on forever. The town cathedral and a tequila factory stand adjacent to one another. Almost every building in town, except the cathedral, is festooned with tequila advertisements and brand names. The land is arid, and dominating the horizon is a dormant volcano. Virtually all of the town's 17,000 inhabitants depend upon the tequila industry for their livelihood. The town's largest hotel has ten rooms.

Yet, touring the fields and factories, one is quickly caught up in the feeling of pride and tradition that is much a part of a thriving industry literally scratched by hand from the parched hillsides. The Sauza firm maintains a small museum in the town of Tequila, tracing the industry's history as well as its own. Among the many displays is a collection of pre-Columbian artifacts found by workers in the maguey fields, stone implements, pottery, ceramic figures, and jade carvings.

In the old days, the harvested maguey hearts were cooked in the open fields in deep, stone-filled pits, then carried by burro to crude distilleries, where they were crushed by round, burro-driven stone presses. The tableau is rich in imagery: the sweet, honey smell of the plant's burning juices; white vapors hanging ghostlike in the afternoon heat; the bray of the burros, the creak of wagons.

Today, in gleaming distilleries, the maguey hearts are split open and steamed in ten-ton pressure cookers. The resulting liquid flows into large steel vats for fermentation, which takes forty-eight to seventy-two hours. After a double-distillation process that requires two weeks or more, a potent 110-proof tequila emerges.

This colorless "silver" tequila is then reduced with distilled water to the desired proof, generally 96 proof for Mexican consumption, 80 to 86 proof for the U.S. market.

Some tequila is set aside for aging. An amber-colored tequila is produced by aging the liquor in oak barrels for about four years. Although of far superior quality, the dark or "gold" tequila is often passed up by consumers who assume that the clear product is better, a problem long familiar to rum producers.

Tequila is traditionally consumed straight, in the classic manner: pour a little salt on the back of your hand just beneath the thumb, lick the salt, down the tequila, then chew on a lime wedge to cauterize your taste buds. Repeat the process often enough and soon you'll be smiling and dancing across the table tops or singing "Ku-Ku-Ru-Ku-Ku" all by yourself.

East Coast yuppies take the tequila-drinking ritual a step further: they find a willing partner; pour a little salt on his or her neck, shoulder, breasts, chest, or wherever; lick off the salt; kiss the partner (while removing a lime wedge from his or her mouth); bite the lime; and drink the tequila.

Heck, I've been doing it that way for years.

Tequila was virtually unknown in the United States, except in the Southwest border states, until fairly recently. Sales in the United States jumped 2,500 percent between 1975 and 1995, making the United States the world's largest tequila importer and accounting for between 88 and 90 percent of all tequila exports. Canada, France, and Japan are next. More tequila is now exported than is consumed nationally.

Today, several German and Japanese firms are making and marketing a tequila of sorts, and Brazil produces a tequila-like liquor with a tequila-like name—but it's not tequila. Needless to say, such imitators draw the wrath of the Mexican manufacturers, who warn that all authentic tequila bears the initials DNG (Dirección General de Normalidad) on the label, meaning that it meets rigid Mexican government standards and contains no chemical additives.

And, if you believe the ancient Aztecs and their modern descendants, it's also good for what ails you.

Hussong's Cantina

Mexico's version of the saloon is the cantina. Possibly the most famous of all cantinas in Mexico, and surely the wildest, is Hussong's in Ensenada, about sixty miles down the Baja California peninsula from Tijuana.

Founded in 1892 by Percy Hussong, a German immigrant, Hussong's Cantina has remained virtually unchanged over the years, surviving the gold rush, the Mexican Revolution, the death of its owner (relatives took over when Hussong died in 1972; his grandson Roberto now runs the place), and the sweep of progress that has seen Ensenada's population swell from 5,000 when the cantina first opened to more than 200,000 today.

The outside facade of Hussong's is about as imposing as a tailor shop. A sign—Hussong's Cantina—hangs above one for Corona beer. An enterprising dealer sells American-style hot dogs from a cart outside the cantina; no meals are served inside.

Hussong's is usually wall-to-wall people at any time of the day or night, a surprisingly even mix of Mexicans and gringos, who get along fine. If the Mexican-American War was played out again, the armistice would be signed in Hussong's.

The ceilings are of coffered tin. There's a huge fireplace, although no one can remember it ever having been lit. The hand-hewn backbar is of genuine Old West vintage. There's sawdust on the floor and a moose head on the wall. At least it looks like a moose head. It may be a patron.

The place is usually so crowded that customers often double-up on the chairs, while waiters with trays held aloft do a marvelous balancing act. A mariachi band adds to the confusion.

The last time I was there, tequila was seventy cents a shot.

The popularity of Hussong's Cantina is such that it recently began licensing T-shirts, sweaters, beach bags, and the like. A store a few doors away on the corner exclusively handles the merchandise at boutique prices.

El Rey Sol, one of Mexico's oldest and finest restaurants, is located only a few blocks from Hussong's. Despite the best of intentions, many El Rey Sol reservation-holders stop at Hussong's for a before-dinner drink and never make it to the restaurant.

The owners of El Rey Sol understand.

Shopping for Silver

Much of Mexico's tourism appeal is its fabulous shopping—colorful ceramics, baskets, serapes, folk art, fine art, carvings, tinware, textiles, leather goods, antiques, glasswork, and pottery.

But what dazzles visitors most is Mexico's superb silverwork. Reflecting the light of centuries, Mexico's silver jewelry and decorative arts are honed and polished with an infusion of rich and diverse cultures. Ancient Mayan monkey figures dance in lilting symmetry across the broad band of one bracelet, while another shows the influence of classical Spain. A necklace of large silver beads is stunning in its modern-day simplicity. A gleaming table piece shaped in the head of a Toltec warrior, a vase styled in slender elegance.

Mexico is the world's leading producer of silver, mining more than half the world's supply. The early Aztecs of central Mexico and the Zapotec and Mixtec people of Oaxaca considered silver to be more precious than gold. It was harder to extract and more difficult to work. The Aztecs, never at a loss for descriptive phrases, described silver as *itzacteocuitatl,* excrement of the gods.

Mexico's early Indian craftsmen produced exquisitely detailed works of art by using the lost-wax method: A wax model, etched and detailed with a stylus, is made and then coated with a heat-resistant plasterlike material to form a mold. The mold is heated until the wax melts and runs out, after which the molten metal is poured into the vacant mold, forming the final object.

Rich silver mines opened the interior of Mexico to Spanish colonization. In some places, the Spanish shoed their horses with silver because it was more plentiful than iron, which had to be shipped from Spain. A *caballero's* status was measured by the amount of silver he lavished on his horse—saddle decorations, bridle, bit, and stirrup. And on himself—hatband, belt buckle, spurs, buttons, eyeglass frames, and even artificial teeth. In its heyday, Guanajuato was one of the great silver-mining centers of the world. For centuries the export of silver dominated the Mexican economy.

Taxco, located between Mexico City and Acapulco, today forms the epicenter of the nation's silver production. Although its mines have long been depleted, the town's 12,000 residents are almost all involved in one way or another with the crafting, sale, and distribution of silver. Tourism provides the customers who come in droves to this picturesque mountain town. Taxco clings to the Sierra Madre hillsides with a network of narrow, cobbled streets lined with white stuccoed houses with red-tiled roofs. Tropical flowers tumble in clusters from balconies and across shaded walkways.

The center of town is the magnificent church of Santa Prisca, a baroque sanctuary whose altars are ablaze with carved and gilded decorations. Its construction was financed in the eighteenth century by silver baron José de la Borda in thanks for the untold millions of pesos that poured out of the Taxco-area mines, making him one of the wealthiest men of his day.

It was an American entrepreneur, William Spratling (a former Tulane University professor), who began the town's silver workshops in the early part of this century. He hired local youths, taught them silversmithing, and was among the first to integrate pre-Columbian designs into modern jewelry. Today, dozens of these shops are still open, and it is here that skilled artisans, many whose fathers began as barefoot apprentices to Don Guillermo (as Spratling came to be known), craft some of the most beautiful silver pieces in the world. Spratling's former home, just behind the Santa Prisca, is now a museum. Its displays tell the story of the silver industry in Taxco and contain dozens of prized pieces.

Taxco has more than 200 silver shops. Most of the better ones are clustered around the *zócalo* and on Avenida Kennedy, which runs through the center of town. Antonio Pineda (Plaza Borda) and Los

Castillo (Plazuela Bernal 10) are considered by many to be the best. La Mina, a silver shop located in a former silver mine, is certainly the most unique.

Taxco holds an annual silver fair, usually during the last week in November or the first week in December, with prizes going to the best silversmiths, who come from far and wide to show their wares. Accompanying cultural events include performances by popular radio and television stars, good food, music, and fireworks. With its historic church, flowering plazas, and picturesque buildings, Taxco was declared a national colonial landmark in 1928, sealing the characteristic appeal of the city that remains unchanged to this day.

Zacatecas in north-central Mexico is another major silver producer, and mining still shapes the character of the city. The Centro Platero de Zacatecas is a local silver center and school housed in a 300-year-old Spanish colonial building where students from all over the country come to learn the principles of silver production, design, and craftsmanship. The center plans to establish more than 200 classrooms by the year 2000, providing training and jobs for 1,000 or more silversmiths and apprentices.

Cosmopolitan Mexico City is also a major marketplace for top quality silver. Tane (Amberes 70) in the trendy Zona Rosa is considered the Tiffany's of Mexico. Customers are greeted at the door with a red carnation and a bag of chocolates wrapped in silver foil. It's the place to go for the finest in flatware, candlesticks, bowls, picture frames, and jewelry, all at prices to match the store's and the neighborhood's snobbish appeal.

Madero, a colonial street with shade trees, benches, and graceful lampposts located in the old part of Mexico City, near the Zócalo, used to be known as the Street of Silversmiths. Many of the old shops remain, and others can be found along the adjoining pedestrian malls, but the area lacks the cachet of today's more fashionable Polanco district and the Zona Rosa. Most of the shops along the Street of Silversmiths now offer competitive prices, and the owners are open to discreet bargaining.

Not for sale in most jewelry shops but much sought after by collectors are *milagros,* small, delicate silver pieces shaped like hearts, hands, arms, legs, kidneys, or other afflicted parts of the human body. The pious attach these little medals to the robes or skirts of religious statues in church in hope of a cure. *Milagros* are often sold outside of churches. They can also be found in flea markets and antique shops.

Pavillon Christofle, at Galileo 55, is an exclusive, elegant shop carrying the finest in silverware, china, and cutlery. At Amberes 41, is Los Castillos, an outstanding store owned by a well-known Taxco family of silversmiths.

When buying silver in Mexico, whether a simple pair of earrings or a large dinner platter, look for the "sterling" or ".925" stamp required by law. Government regulations are rigid. Sterling must contain .925 parts or more of pure silver and .075 or less of alloy (usually copper in Mexico) to give it strength. Expensive collector pieces may contain additional hallmarks as well such as a Mexican eagle or the name and stamp of the silversmith. Always shop at reputable stores and avoid street and dockside peddlers unless you're in the market for low-priced junk jewelry that looks pretty but in time may turn your wrist, fingers, or earlobes the color of bright, fresh limes.

Unlike the products of England, Denmark, and Sweden, the bulk of Mexican silverwork is handmade and hand-polished. Occasional flaws and striations only add to its beauty.

Cantinflas Remembered

*H*e was a living icon, and I was as awed as a stagestruck teen-ager. Mario Moreno was a sophisticated man of the world who read Shakespeare and Cervantes and piloted his own plane. He agreed to see me for a short meeting. An elegant silk dressing gown covered his tattered costume. He sipped a glass of champagne and leafed casually through an art catalog. He was a quiet, introspective man, who spoke perfect albeit hesitant English in a low, well-modulated voice.

Dining with friends at the elegant Fouquet's in the Camino Real Hotel in Mexico City a few nights earlier, film star Mario Moreno caused hardly a stir among the sophisticated diners, many obviously from the United States and abroad. But back in the kitchen there was pandemonium as workers jostled for a glimpse of the man known to millions as Cantinflas, the best-known, most well-loved comic actor in the Spanish-speaking world.

Before leaving the restaurant, Moreno, aware of the commotion he was causing, went into the kitchen and did a full twenty minutes of pratfalls, smelling, tasting, dropping pot lids, burning his fingers, and crying over onions.

Mario Moreno was eighty-one when he died on April 20, 1993, bringing all the laughter to tears. His films out-grossed all others in Latin America, both domestic and foreign. Most U.S. moviegoers knew him only as Passpartout, David Nivin's ingenious manservant in *Around the World in 80 Days,* or as the impish lead in *Pepe.* But in Latin America no actor was more revered. In a national election he once polled more than 2,000 write-in votes. Children at play imitated his slouching gait and quizzical shoulder shrugs, while adults in smart hotels and small cantinas alike laughed and repeated his latest lampoons of high political figures.

In Mexico City a half-block—long mural by Diego Rivera honors heroes of Mexican history. Cantinflas is the central figure. On holidays, bootblacks along the city's main thoroughfares often dress and grimace like him to drum up business. When he made a public appearance, the government closed all pawn shops in the area, lest the poor hock their meager possessions in order to see him perform.

What made him so popular? In films, Cantinflas was a sad, bedraggled little street bum whose pants, held up by a piece of rope, were forever on the verge of falling down. He wore a battered felt hat, a faded, long-sleeved undershirt that itched, a kerchief around his neck, and a tattered, moth-eaten vest that he treated with the utmost care and respect. His costume was vaguely modeled after that of a Mexican *cargador,* or porter, whose backbreaking work is poorly paid. His small, wistful brown face was painted dead white around the mouth; his eyes were emphasized. A tiny mustache at each end of his upper lip, seemingly daubed on with shoe polish, was as much a trademark as his famous costume, which didn't change in nearly sixty years. ("Of course, I send it out to be cleaned now and then," he said.)

When he talked, his words were often a madcap gibberish, verbal somersaults consisting of ad-libs, double-talk, innuendoes, and words that didn't exist or were mercilessly mispronounced. In Spanish, the verb *"cantinflear,"* inspired by him, means to talk too much while saying too little; the noun form means a lovable clown.

"And for your headache," he would advise a sick friend, "put this salve on your forehead and rub it very hard."

"Will it stop it from hurting?" the friend asks.

"No, but it will make it smooth."

Cantinflas always played the good guy, the schnook, says a friend. He was forever trying to help someone else when what he needed was for someone to help him. But he never asked for help.

A typical Cantinflas gag was to break suddenly into a scene of overwhelming chaos in which monumental disaster was about to occur and cheerfully inquire, "¿Qué tal?" That's roughly the Spanish equivalent of "What's cooking?" It had the typical Mexican audience rolling in the aisles for a full five minutes.

In Romeo y Julieta, as he waxes poetic to his lady love on her balcony from the street below, a scrawny dog comes along and wets his leg.

In his guise of a hardworking porter, most Mexicans saw themselves or people they knew. Because his problems were so tremendous, theirs seemed small by comparison. Humor has strange antecedents—sorrow, misery, hostility, fear. Through a simple and sympathetic portrayal, Cantinflas was able to traverse those emotions, turn them around, and make people weep with laughter.

There was much Chaplin pathos in the comedy of Cantinflas. Like Charlie Chaplin, Cantinflas was a pantomime. He used his hands, eyes, and legs with exquisite timing. He gestured apathetically with his hands, which invariably held a long-ashed cigarette. He walked with a deliberately pompous swagger that contrasted sharply with his ragged clothes and downtrodden personality. The walk was further accentuated by busy, mobile hips that conflicted with the rigidity of the rest of his body. He seemed to be going in two directions at once.

Cantinflas and Chaplin shared many aspects of their lives: a childhood of poverty, early careers in the circus and on stage, and finally, great success in films.

But whereas Chaplin represented frustration, Cantinflas represented triumph. Somehow, despite multiple mistakes, Cantinflas managed to overcome his devastating predicaments. In one sketch he is a well-meaning but fumbling waiter who spills soup down the neck of a cabinet minister, puts his thumb into a society matron's mashed potatoes, and drops her steak on the floor, only to retrieve it with grimy hands. His restaurant prospers nonetheless.

Cantinflas continually satirized topics that Mexicans love most, and high on that list was bullfighting. It was his sixteenth film, Ni sangre, ni arena (Neither Blood nor Sand), a brilliant spoof on the Spanish matador Manolete, that catapulted him to international stardom. In it he played dual roles—that of a pretentious, arrogant matador and that of a humble, devoted fan. Through a classic mix-up of identities, the lowly fan is mistaken for the vain bullfighter and the fun begins.

Cantinflas successfully carried the role of the comic-mimic bull-fighter offscreen as well, and until his later years he was perhaps the only "matador" who could unfailingly fill Mexico City's 50,000-seat Plaza de Toros, the world's largest bullring, time and time again. He was all over the ring, jumping up and down or dancing a mambo or a cha-cha-cha. The bull, following his movements, seemed to stare in amazement. From the moment of his strutting, pigeon-toed entrance through the final minutes of the corrida, the crowd belonged to Cantinflas. When the bull pawed the ground, Cantinflas pawed the ground. He read a newspaper, undaunted, as the bull rushed by. He patted the bull's head or held its tail and around in circles they went. He took a mouthful of water, which is traditionally spit on the ground, and squirted it into his assistant's face. He tumbled into the charging bull's path and somehow es-caped unharmed. His pants fell off, revealing pink, ruffled under-wear, and he scampered red-faced to the nearest refuge for repairs.

The death and drama of the bullring is not the easiest subject to satirize, yet Cantinflas always did it in a way that avoided poor taste. The bull never lost its dignity, nor its life.

The moment of truth for Cantinflas was when he plunged a mock sword over the bull's horns. On contact, it would burst into a brilliant bouquet of flowers. The crowd went wild.

A onetime shoeshine boy, but millionaire at forty, Mario Moreno, the son of José and María Guizar Moreno, was born on August 12, 1911, in a respectable but poor section of Mexico City that has since fallen on even harder times. The sixth child in a family of twelve sons and three daughters, he completed high school but received his most valuable education, singing and dancing, in the streets. As he grew, the restrictions of a well-meaning but domineering father, poverty, and a large family seemed stifling to a youth of his imagi-nation. He was kept at home by the deep love he felt for his mother. At fifteen he was sent to the agricultural school in Chapingo, where he stayed for nine months before running away to the Jalapa. He joined a *carpa,* or tent show, and there he met his wife, a Russian dancer (who died of cancer in 1964 at the age of fifty).

His home, nestled 1,500 feet above Mexico City in the Lomas de Chapultepec suburb, was very much his castle and featured picture windows fifty feet long, a jai alai court, a fully equipped motion picture theater seating 200, a large swimming pool with hand-laid tiles, an exquisite collection of pre-Columbian art (including a prized Aztec calendar stone), and lavish furnishings—all the expected trim and veneer of a phenomenally successful man, plus that sense of privacy and loneliness that always accompanies fame.

He owned two film companies, vast real estate holdings, office buildings, houses in Mexico City and Acapulco, a 2,000-acre bull-breeding ranch in Toluca, and an annual income counted in millions of dollars.

It is said that Moreno, one of the biggest philanthropists in show business, gave more than half of his earnings to charity (causing more than one anguished movie exhibitor to throw up his hands and sigh, "The more he gives to the poor, the higher he raises his fees"). In 1952 Moreno launched a social improvement program in Mexico, pledging to raise $12 million a year for the construction of housing units, hospitals, and clinics. Called Madelana Michuca, the project now has more than 100 buildings and is still growing.

Moreno received thousands of requests a year to do benefits, but after a heart attack in the 1980s, he accepted but a few—and only those benefiting children. He had no children of his own, except for an adopted son, Mario Arturo Moreno.

Since 1936, when first seen in a two-reel movie advertisement for trucks, the character of Cantinflas has remained unchanged. "The audience knows him and is very comfortable with him," said Moreno. "A new suit or even a new pair of shoes would change him completely." Indeed, Cantinflas and his antics are so well known that audiences anticipate his reactions to almost any situation. The laughter starts when his name first flashes on the screen. Among his best-known films were *The Firefighter, Patrolman 777, The Unknown Gendarme,* and *If I Were President.*

Moreno's adopted son received the bulk of his father's consider-

able estate when the actor died, including a ranch, valuable property, several cars, and rights to the nearly fifty films Moreno made
over four decades. The will was contested by Moreno's nephew,
Eduardo Moreno Laparade, who claimed that the actor's son was a
spendthrift who never worked and that he beat the aged comedian
on several occasions when high on drugs.

The Eyes of the Matador

*I*n August 1997, fifty years after his death, he was remembered with a requiem mass in the small, dimly lit bullfighters' chapel beneath the Plaza de Toros in Madrid. All day, young and old alike crowded into the tiny chapel and offered prayers for him before the statue of La Macarena, patron saint of matadors. In Córdoba, where the hawk-faced, sad-eyed bullfighter was born, his grave was covered with flowers.

In Linares, where he died, a corrida was held in his honor, with two of Spain's leading matadors, Miguel "El Litri" Baez and Enrique Ponce, and from Mexico, Miguel Espinosa Armillita, fighting Miura bulls from the same dreaded stock that took his life. About 10,000 spectators packing the bullring held a minute of silence and then threw carnations into the ring before the fight began. It was televised worldwide.

And in the Spanish press, where critics had once alternately praised and rebuked him, there appeared sad nostalgic accounts of his life and his death on August 29, 1947.

In those brief, fleeting years between boy and man, Manuel Rodríguez y Sánchez, known as Manolete, became the most famous matador the world has ever known. A tall man, proud, arrogant, and serious, whose daring style and unflinching bravery set the standard against which all other matadors would ultimately be compared, Manolete had just turned thirty when death caught him on the horns of a fat black bull. He has not been forgotten.

Few speak, however, of the silent fear that plagued Manolete through the last years of his life and which may have played a part in his death. He thought he was going blind.

Although the profession that made him a legend was strenuous, Manolete was a frail man. An early illness had left him thin and physically underdeveloped. His father, a second-rate matador also named Manolete, the son and grandson of bullfighters, had such rapidly failing eyesight that he was forced to wear glasses in the bullring toward the end of his career. He became blind when Manolete was only five. Leading his sightless father through the narrow, crowded streets of Córdoba was a memory that remained strong in Manolete's mind. Penniless, the father lived out his few remaining years in a pitiful existence, led about by a child whose own sad eyes appeared far older than his years.

After his father's death, his mother married another bullfighter. Much of Manolete's childhood was thus spent on the bull ranches and in the dusty country rings in and around Córdoba. There it was that his love for bullfighting was first nurtured, and his early skill with the cape quickly became apparent. In 1935, at the age of seventeen, he became a *novillero,* and after the Spanish Civil War, he became a full-fledged matador de toros. He made his debut in 1942 in the bullring of Seville, Spain's most beautiful plaza, and was immediately acclaimed as a great torero, praised for his steel nerves and his pure classic style. His slim, brooding good looks caught the attention of many Andalusian beauties, and Manolete became the rage of Spain.

But after a while, bullfighting aficionados grew bored. Manolete's great skill made bullfighting seem so simple that they demanded more and more of him. They preferred reckless daring to perfection. They wanted tricks, not flawless control.

"It is for that that I am Manolete," he said, after his unshakable bravery had led to a vicious goring in a Mexico City bullring. "It is for that that I charge what I charge."

In 1946, his second tour of the plazas of Mexico and South America was going successfully enough when he suddenly cut it short and returned to Spain. He had been away for four months—during which time he became some $250,000 richer—but those months seemed to have drained him of his spirit. He was not the same man. Since childhood, his immobile face and large, expressionless eyes had always belied his youth, but now there was no mistaking the lines of age that were etched into his coppery skin. At twenty-nine, gray streaked his hair, and his lithe body bore the scars of many near disasters. Exhausted, he began to speak quietly of retirement.

But rest would not come. Like the proverbial gunslinger of the Old West, there was always a younger man anxious to obtain the title of Número Uno. Twenty-one-year-old Luis Miguel Dominguín, who had already proclaimed his challenge, was being hailed as the new great man of bullfighting. And there was the brilliant Carlos Arruza of Mexico.

Manolete began to drink. He didn't drink heavily, but because he had never taken alcohol before, his friends became alarmed. Perhaps, they hoped, only alcohol had caused the dream a month or so before his death from which he awoke screaming that he couldn't see. He stumbled about in his darkened hotel room until his manager came from a nearby room to quiet him.

But the story got out, and it persisted.

A reporter from the local paper heard that Manolete, like his father before him, was losing his vision. On the scent, he came to the matador's room.

"About his eyes, is it true?" the reporter asked.

Antonio Torgores, a popular young matador from Mexico whom Manolete had befriended and who was traveling with him, stood at the window at the far side of the room.

The reporter, reacting to the sudden quiet his question brought into the room, repeated sharply. "Is it true?"

No response.

Finally, the shrewd Camará, Manolete's manager from the beginning, ventured to speak. "Señor, you are a fine fellow," he said. "It is true. Two weeks ago in Madrid, when Manolete was tossed by a bull, it did something to his back, his spinal column—a pinched nerve, whatever." He glanced at Manolete, who continued to dress through the intrusion. "But there is much sight in his eyes now."

"Is there?" The reporter motioned Manolete to the window. "What does it say, matador? Read it. That sign across the street."

"Mi amigo," said Manolete. He spoke slowly, patiently. "When there is only an hour before the bulls, one does not care for games like this."

"Just read it, Señor."

A look of grave concern crossed Manolete's face, but it lingered for only a moment. "Please, there is little time. I must prepare myself." He started for the door at the far side of the room.

"That sign," said the reporter. "It's one of your own posters. You can't even recognize your own poster."

Manolete stopped at the door, impatience in his eyes. "Please, not now. I will meet you after the bulls. We'll talk about my eyes, my ears, anything you like." Then Manolete smiled one of his rare smiles, a smile that could provoke thousands of cheers in the arena. It said that no harm would ever come to Manolete.

Camará followed Manolete through the door, and the reporter turned finally to Torgores. "Why do you make trouble?" the young matador asked, addressing the reporter without looking at him. "Why do you talk about his eyes?"

The reporter seemed suddenly confused. "Maybe it's not his eyesight at all," he said. "Maybe all that he's lost is his courage."

"Courage?" said Torgores. "All men are afraid. But the brave face their fears."

"A real man is never afraid."

"Sit down, Señor. I will show you. No, no. Sit there." Torgores pointed to the closest chair.

Torgores took a pair of banderillas from the top of the dresser, a spark of mischief in his expression. He held one of the darts in each hand and walked slowly, catlike, to the table at which the reporter was sitting. He stood high on his toes, his back arched, his arms extended until his body formed a graceful T. The faint smile of a moment earlier remained as he stabbed downward with the banderillas.

The reporter flinched, and the point of a banderilla bit into the side of his wrist. When the blood appeared through his shirt-sleeve, the reporter began to groan.

Torgores stepped back, laughing. "It's only a scratch. You moved, Señor. If you had not moved, if you had had courage, you would not have been hurt."

The following month, Manolete accepted Luis Miguel Dominguín's challenge. They met in the town of Linares in southern

Spain. Manolete's second bull of the day was a Miura bull, from the same deadly family of bulls that had claimed the lives of such well-known matadors as Pepete, Espartero, Faustino Posada, Domingo del Campo, and Pedro Carreño.

A bold beauty, the bull tossed its angry head high into the air as it raged from darkness into light across the fine white sand of the arena. It crashed with tremendous force into the fence at the far side of the ring. It turned, startled, confused by the noise, then charged again. Its huge shoulders tapered into a slender, muscular rump, and it moved straight and hard, dividing the ring just as the sun and shadow divided it.

Manolete could have made quick work of this raging animal, but instead, he chose to thrill the crowd, as he had done so many times before. When the moment of truth came, he took the bull head-on, approaching directly over the horns with his sword. He leaned into the blade and felt the point bite into the base of the bull's lowered neck. As he drove down hard against the brutal pressure on his wrist, the bull, at the same moment, tossed its head, its horns ripping savagely into Manolete's groin.

Tragically, Manolete died the next morning at twelve minutes past five while receiving his fifth blood transfusion.

"I cannot see," were his anguished last words.

I was in France when Manolete was killed in Linares. I first heard the news over the radio. At first, I thought my mind was playing tricks on me. Then the details came across on all the stations as I turned from one to the other searching for the awful truth. I cried. I'm not ashamed to say it, because Manolete merited my tears. Days later, when I was in Córdoba, that same pain came back to me. I left at his tomb the finest bunch of flowers I could find and the most fervent prayers that have come from my lips. May the Virgin of Guadalupe to whom Manolete prayed in Mexico guide him to the Great Power.

Matador Carlos Arruza
Mexico City, February, 1948

The Last American Matador

*D*iego O'Bolger's suite at the Fray Marcos Hotel is far too small for the dozen or so people who have come to visit him before his Sunday fight at the Nogales bullring. Visiting a matador while he dresses in his suit of lights is a ritual as old as bullfighting itself, something akin to visiting a gladiator or a knight of old as he prepares to go into battle.

The room is tacky. Despite fresh paint and flowery new drapes, the rooms at the Fray Marcos seem to sag under half a century of restless nights, soiled sheets, and sweat. I wonder if the same suites are always reserved for touring matadors. Could this be the same room where I once called upon Carlos Arruza or the great gypsy matador Luis Procuna? It seems smaller.

During the peak years, when Dominguín was on the cover of *Life* magazine and Hemingway glorified the corrida, bullfights took place nearly every week in the border bullrings during the Easter-to-October season, attracting huge crowds from both sides of the border. I remember seeing John Wayne and his buddy Ward Bond at one Nogales bullfight. They were mobbed by fans after the fight, a towering Wayne patiently signing autographs for all who asked. Author Barnaby Conrad was a frequent visitor. ("Remember those hot, sticky nights in Acapulco," he scribbled in the book of one delighted University of Arizona coed.) Today, the Nogales ring averages two or three bullfights a year, often charity events, drawing minor bullfighters and small crowds who pay the $10 shady-side general admission in hopes of seeing some spark of that past excitement.

O'Bolger grew up in Tucson, and although he has lived in Coyoacán, a residential suburb of Mexico City, for nearly twenty years, he has a strong local following, including now-grown friends from Salpointe Catholic High School who knew him when his name was James Bolger. He changed it when he moved to Mexico, riding there from Tucson on a BSA 250 British-made motorcycle, which was promptly stolen. He adopted "O'Bolger" from the original Irish; Diego is Spanish for James. The handsome young gringo with the Irish smile became a full-fledged matador de toros on August 17, 1969, at the Plaza Monumental in Tijuana, Mexico's third-largest bullring, following a string of often bloody though always spirited *novilladas,* or apprentice bullfights. He has gone on to fight successfully throughout Mexico, Spain, and South America and in numerous bloodless bullfights in the U.S. Southwest.

There have been many American bullfighters—Harper Lee, Sydney Franklin (the "Bullfighter from Brooklyn," Hemingway's friend), and John Fulton, as well as female bullfighters Bette Ford and Patricia McCormick. Not long ago, David Renk of San Antonio drew a flurry of interest—and a major piece in *Sports Illustrated*—but quickly faded from the scene. O'Bolger remains, the last American matador. With bullfighting on the wane—the art of dying is literally a dying art—there may never be another of his stature. A small but vocal movement in Spain labels bullfighting cruel and is attempting to have it banned. Animal protection groups in Mexico have had some success, recently closing several bullfighting schools there. Television, once heralded as a boon to bullfighting, has done little to increase interest. The drama simply doesn't translate well to the small screen.

When I arrive at O'Bolger's room, his jacket is folded neatly on the bed, and he is shirtless. Visiting a freshly showered, superbly conditioned half-naked matador in a dinky hotel room would seem a ritual tailored more for adoring young ladies than for men. But the Mexican machismo—cigar-chomping and back-thumping *abrazos*—gives it a benign locker-room atmosphere that is almost comical.

Unlike Arruza and Procuna, whose bodies bore the signs of

many injuries, O'Bolger has no noticeable scars on his upper torso. At six feet, one of the tallest matadors ever, his major wounds have been below the waist. He was once hospitalized for five days after being gored in the left thigh. He was also severely gored in the right calf. To stay in shape, he trains daily in Mexico City, jogging in the hills above Chapultepec Park for as much as ten miles a day, or until occasional nosebleeds—caused by the 7,350-foot altitude and polluted air—force him to stop.

Tall, slim, and good-looking, with none of the hawkish features so common among bullfighters (Manolete's legacy), O'Bolger gets dressed while greeting friends there to wish him success with the afternoon's corrida and discussing last-minute details with ring officials. The limousine that is supposed to take him to the arena has been booked for a funeral; he'll have to find some other way to get there. He orders tea from room service. "Would anyone like something to drink?"

When the tea arrives, O'Bolger takes the tray and puts it aside, never touching it. He puts on his frilled white blouse, leaving the cuffs unbuttoned. Then he puts on a thin red tie, twisting a small loop of thread to the base and tucking it into his trousers. The last thing a matador needs in the bullring is a red tie flapping in the breeze.

The matador's elaborately embroidered suit is like no other. Its origins date back to the 1700s, when the suits were sewn with real gold threads that glistened in the sun. Surely the suit would seem out of place in any ordinary closet. When not in use, it's probably folded away in a trunk, like a trousseau, waiting for its inevitable date with the bulls. Spanish artist Joan Mora sculpted a suit of lights in bronze—*La silla del toreo*—the life-sized jacket is draped over the back of a chair, the trousers are folded across the seat, the cap sits on top. Salvador Dalí once staged a surrealistic bullfight in Barcelona; his matadors wore costumes with thousands of little mirrors sewn onto them so that the bulls, horns painted blue and gold, could see themselves attacking.

The matador's skintight pants, *teleguillas,* are nearly impossible to put on single-handedly. Assistants often have to help the bullfighter squeeze into them, something that's obviously done before visitors begin to arrive. If the matador has knobby knees, a few wraps of newspaper may be added for a smoother look. The pants are no easier to remove. There's no such thing as even the briefest of dalliances—a quickie—for a man in a suit of lights. The real sexual overtones take place in the bullring, where the matador, strutting his prowess and courage, flaunts his maleness to the ultimate point of plunging his sword into the conquered bull.

The others in the room are mostly friends from Tucson, including an attractive female photographer with enough cameras around her neck to photograph the Olympics. Women are considered bad luck in a matador's dressing room, but clearly she's a friend. The tea, it turns out, is for her.

She was working in the hotel room, Nikon poised and ready. O'Bolger goes to the dresser—where he had earlier unrolled a small, beige mat—and places upon it a silver cross, a candle, and a framed postcard-sized picture of the Virgin of Guadalupe. He lights the candle, makes a sign of the cross, and with his head bowed, says a silent prayer. I suspect the gesture may be more for show than a plea for spiritual intervention. He could have said his prayers before the room was full of people, cameras clicking away.

Prayers finished, O'Bolger pulls on his jacket—his suit of lights is green, of course, for his Irish heritage—running his fingers lightly over the sleeve's flowered embroidery. More pictures.

Also on hand is local bullfight guru Dick Frontain, who writes for various bullfighting publications, helps promote scheduled bullfights in Nogales, and was the bullfight critic for the *Arizona Daily Star,* back when the fights had a larger following and advertised regularly in the paper.

Frontain teaches English and short-story writing at Pima Community College in Tucson. Each summer, he flies to Spain, checks into Madrid's Hotel Victoria, drinks a cool sherry or two at the Cerveceria Alemana, and attends as many bullfights as he can squeeze into his three-week stay. Back home, he occasionally ventures into the ring to make a few passes with young bulls during amateur bullfighting events, or during *tientas* at the Trincheras

Ranch of Sonoran friends, a feat perhaps accomplished with more grace and agility before his hair turned white.

I had met O'Bolger for the first time at Frontain's home in Tucson the night before. I knew who he was, of course—anyone who follows bullfighting would know, especially in Tucson. But we had never met. He had arrived at the party with a stunning young woman who turned out to be the photographer doing a story about him.

"Do you think Diego's having it on the photographer?" I asked Frontain. He appeared genuinely surprised at my question. "No way," he said. "He's engaged to a girl in Mexico City. Delfina something. He's crazy about her."

The Plaza de Toros in Nogales was built in 1952 and has gone through various owners and transformations. Closed for several years, it was converted briefly into a brassiere factory. Current impresario Paco de la Fuente, who lives in Mexico City, acquired the ring in 1983. He has poured considerable investment into the 5,000-seat arena—new paint, restrooms, and a new *barrera,* the wooden fence that encircles the ring (vandals carried off the old one for fire and building wood)—but he has not yet been able to show a profit. The ring acquisition included an adjacent rundown apartment house, which de la Fuente would like to demolish. He wants to build a restaurant and a pavilion and expand parking facilities, but the apartment tenants are protected by local housing laws, and de la Fuente is unable to force them out.

Earlier in the day I had gone with Frontain to the *sorteo,* or drawing of the bulls, at the corrals behind the bullring. Here the matadors, appearing shorter and somewhat less magnificent in street clothes, get their first look at the bulls they'll be fighting that day and, if they haven't already met, of one another. The matadors, or their designated representatives, draw numbers to determine which bull or bulls they'll be facing. The numbers are written on cigarette papers, crumpled into tiny balls, and drawn from a hat. As with everything else in bullfighting, the *sorteo* is a serious ritual. Attending it is an honor, an insider's gig, so there is endless posturing, handshaking, and bravado. Owner Paco de la Fuente was there. He and Frontain, both wearing long-sleeved guayabera shirts, embraced, as though they hadn't just met and talked outside an hour earlier.

While one bull looks pretty much like every other bull to the unskilled observer, bullfighters and aficionados can wax on forever about subtle nuances—the shape of a horn, color, size, the set of the neck and shoulders. Bullfighters are notoriously superstitious and easily spooked. The mere cast of a bull's eye can be unsettling, a sign of doom. "Mexican bulls tend to be shorter and slimmer than those in Spain," said Frontain. "But they're strong, fast, and deadly with their horns."

After the bulls were assigned, we headed to Elvira's for *chiles rellenos.* O'Bolger went back to the hotel. Traditionally, bullfighters don't eat before a fight. If the worst happens and surgery is required, the doctors don't want to have to go digging through a lot of tamales and beans to make repairs.

O'Bolger, in his suit of lights, is driven to the bullring rather unceremoniously in the photographer's van. I ride with Frontain, who saunters through the main gate without paying while I cough up $10 for a ticket. Appearing with O'Bolger is another local favorite, Carlos Gonzales, whose dark Spanish good looks have caught the attention of numerous Sonoran beauties, several of whom I had noticed earlier at the *sorteo,* their high heels sinking into the mud. I also notice that O'Bolger's name is spelled incorrectly on the posters and programs, -ar instead of -er. No big deal, I guess, unless it's your name and you're going out onto the dusty Sunday circle to kill or be killed by a furiously charging 1,250-pound animal bred for no other purpose than to fight.

It's said that the only thing that starts on time in Mexico is the bullfight. A matador generally travels with his own cuadrilla, seconds, and sword handlers who place the banderillas and test the bulls with their capes so the matador can judge the bull's characteristics and possible flaws. But this is a border fight in a border ring, and the banderilleros and picadors are all locals—retired or would-be matadors doing a day's work.

All are gathered now beneath the arena in the passageway that leads to the ring. Greetings are simple among these men, as greetings tend to be when protocol is high, mere nods of acknowledgment. O'Bolger and Carlos Gonzales move to the front of the group and stand waiting behind the wide wooden doors that separate them from the ring. Even the picadors' horses, padded and blindfolded, seem to sense the immediacy; one backs into the wall and takes several moments to settle down. Outside, a faulty loudspeaker announces the arrival of the matadors. Slowly the minutes pass, and then from the other side of the door the anxious rattle of hinges and bolts is heard. Suddenly, the huge wooden door swings open, flooding the passageway with light. O'Bolger shields his eyes for a moment, adjusts his fancy dress capote, and throws his shoulders back. Then, as the metallic notes of "La Virgen de la Macarena" trumpet loud and clear through the warm afternoon air, he walks forward, leading the procession of matadors, banderilleros, mounted picadors, and ring attendants from the narrow, sunken passageway out onto the sun-white sand of the open arena.

Of today's corrida, Frontain would later report:

> As O'Bolger attempted to place his own banderillas, he was caught and tossed high into the air. He landed on the bull's back and fell onto the sand. The crowd screamed as one as the bull slashed at the fallen torero. Because of the blood, many thought O'Bolger had been gored in the face. But the horns missed and his assistants lured the bull away from the fallen matador.
>
> Dazed, half-conscious, O'Bolger was assisted to his feet. His forehead was deeply cut and he was spitting blood. The medical team rushed him to the ambulance outside. But O'Bolger broke free, staggered back into the arena and demanded his muleta and sword. He managed a dozen right-hand passes, often working the horns close to his body. The sword thrust was honestly placed and deep. O'Bolger was awarded both ears and took two laps around the arena to ovations and music.

Epilogue

*D*espite the difficult breakup of our marriage or the logistics involved in visiting my children in a foreign country, I was always grateful that my ex-wife and children had settled in Mexico. A country that has shown such great resilience and healing throughout its own tumultuous history somehow heals the soul of those who live there and those who visit. It is a warm and gentle country, and I grew to love it through the eyes of my children. How proud I was that they spoke three languages fluently—English, Spanish, and German—and that in restaurants they could handle any menu placed in front of them. They could make quesadillas for themselves for breakfast and pop down a jalapeño without flinching. They've learned patience and values; they've responded to and grown in the warm Mexican sun. I'll always thank my former wife for that.

In time Gerta left Mexico, returning to Germany, and eventually Alexandra and Adrian came to live with me.

About the Author

Ron Butler, winner of Mexico's prestigious La Pluma de Plata Award (presented by the President of Mexico for outstanding travel writing), lives in Tucson, Arizona, sixty miles from the border of Mexico, which he crosses frequently. His previous books include *Fodor's Railways of the World* (David McKay), *Esquire's Guide to Modern Etiquette* (Lippincott), *The Best of the Old West* (Texas Monthly Press), and *Fodor's Guide to New Mexico* (Random House). He is a contributor to such publications as *Travel & Leisure, Travel/Holiday,* and *Ladies' Home Journal* (in which he wrote a monthly travel column for three years), and his articles have appeared in major newspapers throughout the country.